ALEXANDER THE GREAT

The Story of an Ancient Life

Everything we know about Alexander comes from ancient sources, which agree unanimously that he was extraordinary and greater than everyday mortals. From his birth into a hypercompetitive world of royal women through his training under the eyes and fists of stern soldiers and the piercing intellect of Aristotle; through friendships, rivalries, conquests, and negotiations; through acts of generosity and acts of murder, this book explains who Alexander was, what motivated him, where he succeeded (in his own eyes) and where he failed, and how he believed that he earned a new "mixed" nature combining the human and the divine. This book explains what made Alexander "Great" according to the people and expectations of his time and place and rejects modern judgments asserted on the basis of an implicit moral superiority to antiquity.

Thomas R. Martin is the Jeremiah W. O'Connor Jr. Professor in Classics at the College of the Holy Cross in Worcester, Massachusetts. He is the author of *Ancient Greece* and (with Ivy Sui-yuen Sun) *Herodotus and Sima Qian*.

Christopher W. Blackwell is the Louis G. Forgione University Professor of Classics at Furman University in Greenville, South Carolina. He is the author of *In the Absence of Alexander: Harpalus and the Failure of Macedonian Authority* and (with Amy Hackney Blackwell) *Mythology for Dummies*.

ALEXANDER THE GREAT

THE STORY OF AN ANCIENT LIFE

Thomas R. Martin
College of the Holy Cross

Christopher W. Blackwell
Furman University

CAMBRIDGE
UNIVERSITY PRESS

CAMBRIDGE
UNIVERSITY PRESS

32 Avenue of the Americas, New York NY 10013-2473, USA

Cambridge University Press is part of the University of Cambridge.

It furthers the University's mission by disseminating knowledge in the pursuit of education, learning and research at the highest international levels of excellence.

www.cambridge.org
Information on this title: www.cambridge.org/9780521148443

© Thomas R. Martin and Christopher W. Blackwell 2012

First published 2012

A catalogue record for this publication is available from the British Library

Library of Congress Cataloguing in Publication data

Martin, Thomas R., 1947
Alexander the Great : the story of an ancient life / Thomas R. Martin, Christopher W. Blackwell.
    pages   cm.
Includes bibliographical references and index.
ISBN 978-0-521-76748-4 (hardback)   ISBN 978-0-521-14844-3 (pbk.)
1. Alexander, the Great, 356–323 B.C.   2. Greece – History – Macedonian Expansion, 359–323 B.C.   I. Blackwell, Christopher W., 1968   II. Title.
DF234.M37   2013
938′.07092–dc23   2012017961

ISBN 978-0-521-76748-4 Hardback
ISBN 978-0-521-14844-3 Paperback

We dedicate this book to our students, who demand that we reconsider the past, and to our families, who are our joy in the present and our best hope for the future.

CONTENTS

ACKNOWLEDGMENTS

We would like to express warm thanks to Beatrice Rehl (Publishing Director, Humanities, Cambridge University Press) for her support and oversight from the beginning of this project, to Amanda J. Smith (recently Assistant Editor, Humanities, Cambridge University Press) who guided us through the process of submission before moving on to new adventures, to Ken Karpinski (Senior Project Manager, Aptara) for his clear and responsive direction of the preparation of the manuscript for publication, to the anonymous reviewers both for their insightful criticisms pulling no punches and also for their encouraging comments, and to Will Martin, Anne Salloom, and Ivy Sui-yuen Sun for their perceptive assistance in clarifying arguments and in proofreading.

INTRODUCTION: THE GOAL OF THIS BOOK

Ancient writers agree that Alexander was extraordinary, more like a god than a human in everyone's eyes – especially his own. In writing this brief biography for non-specialists, we accept the word of those writers based on what seems plausible to our (necessarily limited) understanding of Alexander's time and place. Our book, therefore, stands on the assumption that the opinions of the ancients must be given great weight, or the story of Alexander's life will make no sense at all. We are therefore diverging from the approach of some prominent modern scholarship on Alexander, especially the opinion that rejects the value of writing the life of such an enigmatic man. We are writing the story of an ancient life.

Guided by that goal, we pay special attention to the ancient Greek literature that Alexander treasured as sources of inspiration and reflection. His knowledge of these texts reached a depth that is difficult for a modern age to appreciate: to the end of his life, whether sober or drunk, he could recognize, quote, and even enact passages from the authors that meant so much to him, especially Homer and Euripides. The surviving remnants of this literature offer clues to the meaning of Alexander's words and deeds, and we have tried to include this evidence often (and there would be still more citations in a longer book!). By emphasizing Alexander's reliance on these texts in understanding his world, his status, and his action, we hope to contribute to a return to a tradition of interpreting Alexander that offers a more source-based view than the modern tendency in some scholarship to see Alexander as little more than a pathological mass murderer.

This biography strives to show that Alexander, like most people of his time and place, viewed proper character as grounded in the hard values of performance, respect, honor, and loyalty. Modern Western ideals of what makes for good character can seem to place less worth on these traits, but Alexander was not a modern man, for better or worse. We have tried to avoid the arrogance of moral judgment that self-righteous modernity can impart. In our considered opinions, people who recall the history of the nineteenth and twentieth centuries, and the course so far of the twenty-first, have little to feel morally superior about compared to other times and places in human history. We sincerely hope that the future will prove Steven Pinker and those who agree with him correct that the "better angels of our nature" are making our world less violent than it was in the past. But, inspired by Alexander and remembering our ancient Greek literature, we dread the *nemesis* that inevitably follows upon *hubris*, the unjustified and self-righteous arrogance in one's moral superiority that is perhaps even more dangerous in the modern world than it was in the ancient.

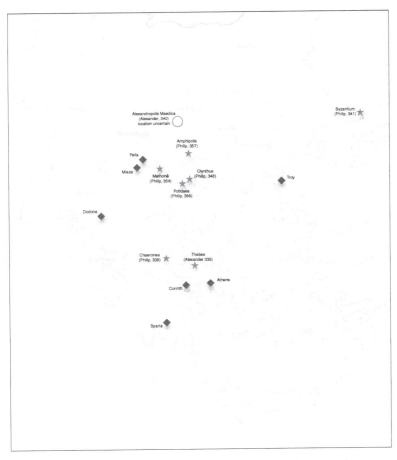

Map 1: European Greece, Macedonia, and Northern Lands

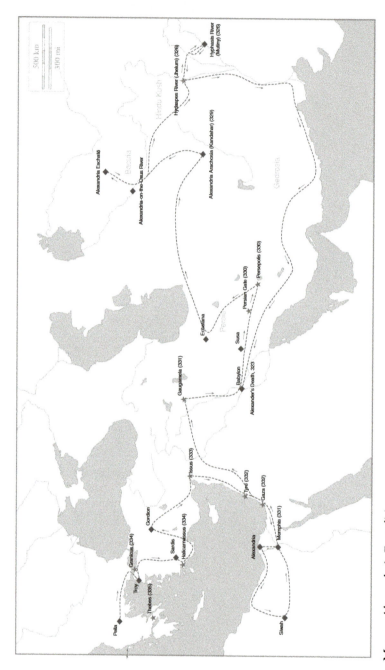

Map 2: Alexander's Expedition

1

THE WORLD OF ALEXANDER'S BIRTH AND HIS EDUCATION IN LITERATURE AND WARFARE (350S AND 340S BC)

§ 1.

Timeline of Alexander's Life

359 BC   Philip II becomes king of the Macedonians.
356 BC   Alexander is born to Olympias and Philip II.
338 BC   Philip II and Alexander defeat the Greek alliance at the battle of Chaeronea.
336 BC   Philip II is assassinated, and Alexander becomes king.
335 BC   Alexander destroys Thebes for rebelling.
334 BC   Alexander begins his expedition to conquer Asia.
333 BC   Alexander defeats the Persian king at the battle of Issus.
332 BC   Alexander captures Tyre after a long siege.
331 BC   Alexander is crowned Pharaoh in Egypt; he defeats the Persian king again at the battle of Gaugamela.
330 BC   The Persian palace at Persepolis is destroyed in a fire for which Alexander is responsible.
329 BC   Alexander reaches Bactria (present-day Afghanistan).
328 BC   Alexander kills Cleitus in a drunken argument.
327 BC   Alexander marries Roxane, daughter of a Bactrian ruler.
326 BC   Alexander's army at the Hyphasis River refuses to march any farther east into India.

324 BC   Alexander returns to Persia by marching through the Gedrosian Desert; Alexander and many of his commanders marry Persian brides at Susa.

323 BC   Alexander dies in Babylon.

Alexander was born in the year 356 (all dates are BC, unless otherwise indicated) in Macedonia, the region of mountains, plains, and rivers between Greece (to the south and east) and the even more mountainous Balkan regions (to the north, west, and northeast). A royal family ruled Macedonia, and Alexander's father Philip ruled as king of the Macedonians. To keep his power, a Macedonian king had to rally support continuously from the fiercely proud leaders dominating the region. These leaders believed themselves to be the social equals of the royal family, and each had many local men ready to follow him into battle. To remain successful, a king of the Macedonians had to win an ongoing competition for status among this social elite. Philip and his ancestors sought legitimacy for their royal standing through their claim that they shared the same ethnic heritage as the Greeks. Most Greeks of the time disagreed, seeing Macedonians as barbarians. For Greeks, barbarians were defined as people who did not speak Greek; barbarians could be brave or noble, but in the competition for cultural and personal status over others that defined Alexander's world, barbarians were, for Greeks, by definition less elite.

For Greeks, Alexander's mother, Olympias, was also a barbarian because she was from Epirus to the west of Macedonia. But Olympias was royal (and rich), from a family that claimed descent from Achilles, made famous by Homer's *Iliad* as the best of the Greek warriors at the time of the Trojan War. Philip's family, too, was royal and very ancient, descended from Heracles (called Hercules by the Romans). Heracles was the most famous human being in the Greek world; literature told of his struggles and victories over enemies, monsters, and gods, and of the prize he won: he became a god after his death, worshipped across the world. Both Achilles and Heracles had a divine parent; Heracles was the son of Zeus, the king of the gods. We must accept that

Alexander, like almost everyone else, believed this heritage to be literally true and monumentally significant. His family history therefore gave Alexander a social status in his world second to none, a fact that was fundamental to his understanding of his life and what he should do with it.

§2.

Alexander was born when Philip was away fighting a war to strengthen his kingdom by taking away from Athenian control the Greek city-state of Potidaea, east of Macedonia. Athens was still a powerful city-state famed for its architecture and literature, but Philip had built Macedonia into a power far greater. He was winning the competition with the Greek city-states for international status and power. On the day Philip's army captured Potidaea, he received news of three other victories: his general Parmenion had defeated the Illyrians, Macedonia's most dangerous northern neighbors; his racehorse had won first place at the Olympic Games, the most prominent competitive festival in ancient Greece; and one of his several wives, Olympias, had born him a son to be his heir to the throne. By taking Potidaea, Philip seized control of that region's gold and silver mines; these rich new sources of precious metals bankrolled Philip's expansion of power. The Illyrians had almost destroyed the Macedonian kingdom several years earlier; defeating them marked Philip as an unquestioned success in the competitive world of Macedonian politics. Given that only Greeks could compete in the Olympics, Philip's victory there earned him the right to boast that he belonged to the Greek elite. The birth of Alexander finally gave him a son he could hope to mold into a successor, keeping Philip's family line competitive in the violently dangerous world of Macedonian royal politics. The court prophets told Philip that his son's birth date, contemporary with his three great victories, meant that the boy would grow up to be "unbeatable, invincible" (*aniketos*).

People at the time, and for centuries after, said that the gods sent signs that Alexander's birth would change the world and that he was no ordinary human being. Olympias had dreamed – most people at the time thought dreams were messages from the gods – that her womb was struck by a thunderbolt from Zeus. Philip dreamed his son would have the nature of a lion. He also claimed that, months before, he had glimpsed a giant snake, surely a god in disguise, sleeping with Olympias; the priest of the god Apollo publicly confirmed the interpretation. On the very day Alexander was born, Persian priests, the so-called Magi, who were visiting the Greek city Ephesus in Asia Minor (present-day Turkey), suddenly panicked when the temple of the goddess Artemis burned down. They ran through the streets shouting that the kingdoms of Asia were destined to fall.

§3.

Alexander began his life in a world of women. Macedonian kings were polygamous, with each wife representing a political alliance with an important family, inside or outside the kingdom. Olympias' homeland, for example, was strategically important for Macedonian security; good relations with the Epirote royal family protected Macedonia's western flank. By the time Philip died, he had married seven women. The political necessity of these marriages did not rule out love; Philip is said to have fallen hard for Olympias when he met her at an international religious festival. Royal women were in charge of their own living space in their homes and palaces; men entered rarely and only with permission. This feminine world was just as competitive as the world of men. The king's wives competed to be the most important, and a child's rank depended on the mother's prominence as well as on the child's own ability in the father's eyes. A child's success would elevate a mother's status.

As a child, Alexander lived among female relatives, friends, and many slaves. Olympias had brought slaves with her from Epirus to Macedonia, while others – working for the royal family as cooks, cleaners, gardeners, musicians, weavers, and in nearly every other trade imaginable – were either born to slaves or were prizes of conquest. Some were northern barbarians with no formal education; others were Greeks, some of whom could read and write and even serve as teachers for children. All of these slaves were property; they could be physically or sexually abused or even killed if their owners were cruel. One of the most important jobs of the women in any wealthy house was to train and manage the household slaves and even to nurse them back to health after sickness or injury. Despite their wide differences in status, royalty and slaves lived closely together in an intercultural and multilingual domestic community. Alexander heard many languages as a child; his mother spoke Epirote, the language of Epirus; his nurse, a free woman from an elite local family, spoke Macedonian, a language related to Greek but incomprehensible to Greeks; various slaves spoke the languages of their native lands. Greek was the common language, and Alexander grew up bilingual in Macedonian and Greek.

A mother's most important duty was to launch her child's education, especially to prepare him or her to enter society beyond the restricted circle of childhood. For Alexander, that was the society of the royal court. Like the world of women, the Macedonian court was strongly international, where Greeks and other non-Macedonians, including Persians, lived as long-term guests. For at least half a century before Philip, Macedonian kings had paid for leading Greek artists, writers, and thinkers to be part of life at court. At the end of the fifth century, the famous Athenian author of tragic dramas, Euripides, was hired to live in the capital city of Pella and write and direct plays in Greek of the kind that thrilled international audiences in Athenian drama festivals. Early in the fourth century, a Macedonian king invited a student of the famous Athenian philosopher Plato to live at court, empowering him with the sensitive job of choosing guests invited to eat at the king's dinner table based on their education in philosophy and geometry.

§4.

The ancient writers say that even before Alexander entered the world of adult men, he loved the broad range of Greek literature:

tragic and comic plays, histories of Greeks and barbarians, philosophical essays on the nature of the world and how people should live in it, and poems honoring victors in war, sports, and politics. To understand Alexander's motivations and goals, it is crucial to appreciate what Greek literature meant to him and his peers. For them, stories of heroes and gods were records of history, not fiction. "Myth" is the Greek word for story, and what we today refer to as "mythology" – a term implying made-up legends – was seen as the complex narrative of genuine interactions between gods and humans in the past. Myths were real for Alexander, and they had meaning beyond entertainment. The stories described competing, even contradictory, versions of the past because history was complicated and meaningful on multiple levels; it was the responsibility of a myth's audience to unravel the significance of this competition of meaning through hard study, deep reflection, creative imagination, and spirited discussion.

For members of the highest social elite, myths taught lessons about their ancestors, reaching back to the beginning of history and the birth of the gods. Zeus, the king of the gods, headed the lineage of Alexander's family, many generations in the past. The stories of Greek literature for Alexander therefore concerned his heritage; they described who he was and prescribed how he should live. It mattered tremendously to Alexander to know what his ancestors had done, and how he could live up to and then go beyond their glorious achievements. His inherited place in the world and his proper role in it, then, were explicable to him only through the lens of literature's stories; these stories were key to Alexander's constructing his personal identity and status. His immersion in Greek literature and passion for knowledge did not make him dreamy or bookish; they reflected his insatiable curiosity, brilliant intelligence, and rigorous education as a member of the upper class of his time and place.

For Alexander, literature revealed guiding principles of life – often harsh and violent and always competitive – that he never forgot. For example, the poems of Pindar from the city of Thebes taught Alexander that a man's greatest victories will disappear and perish unless sung, told, or written down. Alexander learned the dramas of Euripides by heart, their rhythmic lines encapsulating for him and his peers razor-sharp insights into honor and insult that they could hurl at each other like weapons. The most important author of all for Alexander was the poet Homer. His *Iliad* focused on Alexander's ancestor Achilles, the "best of the Greeks." It showed that Achilles lived "always to go beyond others," and therefore chose a glorious death over safety and obscurity. In his quest for immortal fame, he demanded absolute loyalty from others and public recognition of his superior status.

Everything Alexander learned as he grew up described human life as ultimately dependent on the plans of the gods. In ancient polytheistic religion, there was no single set of beliefs or doctrines shared by everyone about the role of the gods and supernatural forces in the lives of people, and there was no organized religious authority to dictate beliefs. Worship at temples and rituals at festivals were important events in all communities, but people also believed that they might meet or talk to the gods at any time, anywhere – if the gods chose to send a message about what human beings should do. Understanding communications from the gods was very difficult, and the stakes could be as high as life or death. People realized that they could never hope to understand fully the nature of the gods; divine majesty was so vastly superior to the position of mere mortals that the gods' plans were by nature incomprehensible. People also knew that to misunderstand what the gods wanted from them was to risk destruction. The gods did not love human beings, nor did they automatically and always want to protect them. Communities and individuals were obliged to honor and worship the gods, with the hope (but not the guarantee) of receiving divine help in return for frequent prayers and sacrifices, especially of large and expensive animals.

The gods were frightening and dangerous, and people prayed to them, sacrificed animals to them, and gave them gifts to avoid their anger. But people also prayed, sacrificed, and gave to the gods out of gratitude. The gods could be the sources of great blessings – children, health, victory, food, wine. Some rituals of worship promised believers a better existence after death. Olympias and Philip met at just such a religious gathering. All accounts say that Olympias was devoted to prayer, sacrifice, and other devotional rituals. She emphasized particularly the worship of Dionysus, who would be a very important god to Alexander throughout his life. Dionysus was the Greek deity who most strongly displayed complexity and ambiguity. Born on earth from a sexual encounter between a woman and the king of the gods, then either torn to pieces by monsters and resurrected or born a second time from the leg of his father, he was a god who had been human at some point in his creation but then became divine. He was the source of great pleasures (wine and sex) for human beings, but also pain and violent death for anyone who showed disloyalty to him or failed to respect his power. Olympias believed that a god had impregnated her and that Alexander was the son of a divine father; eventually, when Alexander was old enough, she told him so.

The gods spoke to people through specially designated priestesses and priests at various sacred places called oracles. Zeus spoke from an oracle at Dodona in western Greece, whereas the Egyptian god Ammon (whom the Greeks thought to be Zeus) answered suppliants' questions at Siwah in the Egyptian desert. The most famous Greek oracle was Apollo's sanctuary at Delphi in central Greece (the oracle Philip consulted after seeing the snake in his wife's bed). The messages of oracles were difficult to understand because they were usually expressed as riddles or obscure hints; other kinds of divine communication – the appearance of particular kinds of birds, dreams, or signs in the sky – were even more obscure. Interpreting all these divine messages and signs required the help of experts.

§ 5.

These were all things that Alexander learned in the world of women where he lived for the first years of his life and from the

Greek literature that he read and discussed at home. When he was old enough and strong enough, perhaps seven or eight years old, he took his first steps into the world of men. In the company of other boys, Alexander trained his body for strength and speed. They ran 200-yard sprints – the length Greeks called a *stadion* ("stadium") – lifted rocks and weights, and began to learn to fight. Through fighting Alexander and his classmates learned strength, speed of hand, foot, and eye, aggression, and how to take pain without panic. This early combat training resembled modern mixed martial arts: punching, grappling, kicking. The ultimate form of ancient fighting was the *pankration*, "total power fighting." The *pankration* was an opportunity to display courage and endurance while in pain. Later in his life, when Alexander sponsored athletic contests, he never encouraged his soldiers to pursue the injury-plagued *pankration*, preferring that they fight with wooden poles, because matches with these mock arms were less likely to disable his troops. Training for war was the constant, obvious goal of Alexander's daily exercises as a boy.

In the world of Alexander's time, war was normal, to defend the home and homeland and to win conquests and riches from others. The frequency of war reflected fundamental assumptions about the nature of human existence. One of those assumptions, shared by Alexander and everyone else, was that individuals and nations were not automatically entitled to an equal claim to status, power, and prosperity. Everyone had a rank, superior to, equal to, or inferior to others. People regularly disagreed about who was entitled to be superior and who had to be inferior, and one function of war was to settle such disputes, at the expense of the freedom of the losers. Those who believed themselves to be superior felt an obligation to assert their status and demand its recognition from others; those who were inferior yet resisted the power of their superiors faced terrible (and inevitable) consequences for their supposed disloyalty. These hierarchical assumptions were built into society, even into the uniquely radical democracy of Athens, where the free citizens were divided according to status into income-based classes that determined their political opportunities. The hierarchy of strength, courage, and ability was the foundation of order and stability in this world. It dominated how Macedonians saw others, and it was the reason that Macedonians trained their sons to be warriors. They trained to fight to maintain their status and the safety of their land, with weapons and with words. All the sons of the nobility learned to fight; none learned to be deferential.

Alexander began training for war with the shorter and lighter weapons of the infantry: knives and swords. This training extended the lessons of the *pankration*, to fight with courage and cunning when the enemy was only an arm's length away, slashing or stabbing with a sharp-edged weapon. He and his friends also learned to use long-distance weapons, shooting arrows with bows and rocks with slings as light-armed infantry, and then to fight as heavy infantry wearing armor and wielding long thrusting spears. It was important for a commander and king-to-be to have experience of all kinds of infantry weapons and tactics so that he could use his troops to best effect. Above all, however, the son of the king had to be a skilled cavalryman, ready to lead charges in person against the enemy. The horse was the vehicle for a military commander in battle, providing mobility and an elevated point of view over a battlefield. As soon as he was large enough, Alexander learned to ride, practicing maneuvers on horseback at high speeds without stirrups (which would be unknown in Europe for another thousand years). He trained to use a cavalryman's thrusting spear and slashing sword, fighting in coordination with others in massed attacks. Through all this training, Alexander learned how far and how fast armed infantry could march and cavalry could ride over different kinds of terrain. He learned how much men eat and drink on the march and how long their strength can endure while fighting. In the company of his father, Alexander saw engineers developing machines of warfare – catapults, siege-towers, portable bridges – and witnessed negotiations with suppliers of weapons, food, and the other things necessary to keep an army fit to fight. Many of these engineers, artisans, and tradesmen were foreigners. The Greeks of Sicily and the Persians had made advances in the science of attacking walled cities; Illyrians had produced innovations in thrusting spears; Greeks had developed tactics for lightly armed troops attacking more heavily armored troops and operating on steep terrain. Alexander, therefore, had to learn to deal with military experts of diverse origins and knowledge.

Alexander shared this training in the arts of war with the sons of his father's social equals. Their drillmasters were hard men from the most rugged areas of the Balkans and Greece: Leonidas from Epirus (a relative of Alexander's mother) and Lysimachus from Acarnania. Famed and feared for their toughness, these foreigners pushed the boys to their limits. The young noblemen hiked together through the hills, fought with each other with hands and weapons, and dined together after hard days of work. Some of these young men became Alexander's lifelong friends, his Companions (*hetairoi*). "Companions" was a title that Macedonians used with a special meaning: as Alexander learned from reading Homer's *Iliad*, these were the people he could count on to help when he was in mortal danger. Such close friends knew one another's abilities and achievements. Their lives depended on each other, not theoretically, looking toward some future battle, but in a very real way every day. From the earliest stages of their training they measured their skills in the wilds of Macedonia hunting animals, large and small. Pindar had written that Achilles had been killing lions, stags, and boars from the time he was six years old, in the kind of competition that revealed who was the superior man. Alexander and his friends hunted birds with throwing nets, rabbits with stones and arrows, and lions and wild boar with spears. This hunting was serious business, and the boys' lives were in jeopardy whenever they faced a large animal. In confronting an enraged lion, boar, or bear, every youth had to know his role and had to trust his Companions to do the right thing. Macedonian art shows scenes of hunting; the main weapons were spears, but if the animal got past their points, hunters had to rely on short swords. Years later, one of Alexander's closest Companions killed a lion in a hunt, but not before the animal clawed the flesh from his shoulder to the bone. The literature that Alexander loved was full of stories of successful or disastrous hunts. The first of the famous "labors" of Heracles, Alexander's ancestor, was to kill a lion with his bare hands. The Greek historian Herodotus tells of a boar hunt where a badly thrown spear tragically kills the son of Croesus, king of Lydia. Each boy's courage or fear was on display at every hunt, and his skill was easily visible to everyone. A Macedonian noble youth was not allowed to dine with adults until he had killed a wild boar without a net; Cassander, the son of a leading Macedonian general and himself a very capable man and combat veteran, was not allowed to recline at dinner with the men even when he was thirty-five years old, because this one feat of arms had eluded him.

Alexander excelled in this dangerous competition. In fact, the ancient writers tell us, he excelled at everything he attempted. In running, the biographer Plutarch reports, Alexander was fast enough to have competed at the Olympic games. But, Plutarch adds, Alexander scorned those games: "When his friends said, 'You are so fast, why don't you compete at Olympia?' Alexander replied, 'Only if I am competing with other kings.'" Alexander was acutely aware that he was the heir to the kingdom, and that therefore the stakes in every form of competition were highest for him. To be born into a royal family among the Macedonians was to begin a life-and-death struggle; no Macedonian royal could opt out. The reward was kingship, and the cost of failure was death. Alexander's father, Philip, had earned his position as king of the Macedonians, and Alexander knew that the rivals whom Philip had beaten were all dead.

Plutarch

Plutarch, writing in Greek in the early second century AD, composed as one of his many works a biography of Alexander. He lived in the town of Chaeronea, the scene of the world-changing battle in 338 between Philip and Alexander against a Greek coalition. Plutarch's biographies were "parallel lives," pairing famous Greeks and Romans. He paralleled Alexander with Julius Caesar as the two greatest leaders of their worlds. Plutarch declared that his biographies were not "histories" because they did not include detailed descriptions of events. As he said at the start of his biography of Alexander, "an explanation of a person's excellence or badness does not lie entirely in his most famous deeds, but often in a casual action, or a word, or a joke." His task as a biographer, he believed, was to uncover "the evidence of the man's soul."

Plutarch also wrote an essay whose title might be translated "Concerning Whether Alexander had Great Excellence or Great Luck." There, Plutarch argued that Alexander was foremost in excellence because he was guided by philosophical ideas, including a vision of a world in which people of all kinds, from Greeks to barbarians, were valued for their personal excellence.

§6.

The story of how Alexander's father became king gives a clear picture of the violence and danger of royal succession in Macedonia: upon the death of a king, the eldest son of that family expected to become his successor, but this heir would not survive, much less keep his position, unless he could assume control of the army, defend the country, and eliminate rivals. Amyntas III, King of the Macedonians and Alexander the Great's grandfather, died in 370. He left three sons: Alexander II, Perdiccas III, and Philip II. (These Roman numerals are a modern convention to identify kings with the same name; the ancient practice was to identify people by adding their father's name. The "Great" Alexander, the subject of our biography, was Alexander III, but was known as "Alexander, son of Philip.") Each of these men became king for at least a short time, one after another, and each died violently. The eldest son, Alexander II, inherited the throne from his father. At once, he faced a war with the Illyrians – the Macedonians' constant rivals for territory – but it was a fellow Macedonian who killed him, only two years later. The assassin, a man named Ptolemy, became "regent" or caretaker of Amyntas III's second son (Alexander II's younger brother), Perdiccas III, because the boy was too young to rule. As soon as Perdiccas considered himself old enough to rule, he had Ptolemy killed and began to act as king of the Macedonians until he was killed in battle with the Illyrians in 359. Perdiccas' son was only a baby, however, so Perdiccas' younger brother Philip, the baby's uncle, became regent, responsible for defending Macedonia. Macedonia needed defense, since the Illyrians had won victory after victory for years, and their recent slaughter of a Macedonian army and king had put the very survival of all Macedonians at risk. The Illyrian victory made Macedonia look weak, like easy pickings. Macedonian territories were therefore immediately prey to invasions.

Philip had to convince the regional leaders of Macedonia that they could defeat their enemies and that he could show them how. Above all, he had to persuade them to risk their most valuable resource, their men, for a common purpose. At the nightly *symposia,* the hours of heavy drinking, conversing, and arguing that generated social bonding (and sometimes violent drunken clashes) among elite Macedonian men, Philip described a combination of political, strategic, and tactical initiatives that would make the Macedonians unbeatable. It would not be acceptable for regional leaders to make treaties with enemies, nor would it be acceptable for some of them to let others' regions fall, piecemeal. Philip, always alert to the possibility of buying rather than fighting for what he wanted, proposed that he and the other leaders begin by paying off their most threatening neighbors for the moment, gaining time to make military changes that would guarantee their long-term security.

Tactically, Philip proposed training the Macedonian infantry in new methods of fighting on the ground, using an even longer thrusting spear similar to those of the Illyrians. This spear, the *sarissa,* was eighteen feet long, with twelve feet extending ahead of the soldier and six feet behind. It had a sharp, edged point at the front end and a metal spike at the rear that could be braced into the ground or used as a weapon should the *sarissa* break; in dire straits, a broken spear became a staff, and the Macedonian soldier would revert to his original childhood training in stick-fighting. The *sarissa* would not break easily, however, as it was made from the cornel tree (dogwood). This extra-long spear was an innovation in the technology of warfare, but it required rigorous practice. These long spears were most useful in the hands of meticulously trained troops arranged in a carefully spaced order, with up to sixteen spearmen in line behind one another. Soldiers held their weapons with two hands and thrust them toward the enemy without impeding or impaling their comrades in the formation. This armored combat unit, the *phalanx*, resembling a metal porcupine with its sharp spines in the air, had to move swiftly in every direction without losing discipline, orientation, or awareness of the tactical situation. A spearman separated from the formation was easy prey for enemy cavalry or archers.

Philip had seen tactics and weapons like this in action during his own youth. The politics of Macedonian royalty had caused him to live with the Illyrians in the north as a "royal hostage," human collateral guaranteeing that the Macedonians would honor a treaty. Later, Philip was sent as a hostage again, south this time, to the Greek city of Thebes, where he lived in the house of Epaminondas, one of the greatest military tacticians of his age. Philip applied what he had learned during these hostage situations to reorganize and re-energize the Macedonian army. He persuaded the leaders of Macedonia's regions to act together; he unified, re-armed, and re-trained their soldiers; he decisively defeated the Illyrians, preserved Macedonia's borders, and expanded its territory, taking valuable lands and wealth away from enemies and rivals. In short, Philip earned his prominence by demonstrating his merit to other proven, capable men from his social class.

Philip began his rise to power in Macedonia when he was "caretaker" for the previous king's under-age son, his nephew, but it is clear that his own successes secured his position as ruler. Philip's accomplishments made him feel so secure, in fact, that he allowed the young Amyntas, the heir to the kingship by blood, to continue to live as part of the family. If Philip's achievements had not been enough to overcome Amyntas' hereditary claim to rule, the violent rules of competition in Macedonian royal politics would have required that one of the two had to die – and Philip clearly believed it would have been the boy.

§7.

In this society where the king of the Macedonians was required to prove his superiority at every moment, the son of a king was under unimaginable pressure to be the best at everything, every time. This sort of pressure was so great that even the famously tough Spartans excused their kings' sons from the rigorous military training required of all young men there; should a prince fail at any test, the Spartans feared the inevitable crisis of leadership. The Macedonians did not shy away from putting their future leaders to the sternest tests, over and over. By the time Alexander came of age, his Companions, and every Macedonian soldier, knew that he had done what they had done, suffered what they had suffered, and met every challenge better than they had.

Alexander excelled not only in feats of strength, skill, and speed, but also in perception, deduction, and judgment based on close observation. Plutarch tells a story that illustrates how these qualities were revealed early on in Alexander's life. A horse trader from Thessaly, a land famous for horses where Philip had close connections, brought an expensive animal for the king's inspection. The horse was named "Bucephalas" ("Oxhead") and, although a magnificent physical specimen suited to be a superb cavalry mount, seemed completely wild and untamable. Philip was about to send horse and salesman away, when Alexander, still a young teenager, complained out loud at the loss of such a fine beast, making it clear that he thought that the older men were too scared to ride the horse. Philip accused his son of impertinence to his elders, whereupon father and son made a bet – if Alexander tried and failed to ride Bucephalas, the boy would pay the horse's purchase price, thirteen talents of silver (a huge amount of money). In fact, Alexander had noticed that the horse was frenzied because he was shying away from his own shadow; leading the animal to face the sun, with its shadow now hidden behind it, Alexander calmed the horse, mounted, and rode across the field and back. Plutarch says that Philip wept for joy, telling his son, "You will have to find your own kingdom to rule; Macedonia will be too small."

This story describes a competition, pitting Alexander against a horse, against the grown Macedonian men, and, especially, against his father. The youth pitted his judgment against that of his elders and won, based on an ability to observe what others did not see. He trusted his judgment and acted on it, making a bet for a huge sum – approximately the equivalent of 200 years' wages for a soldier or a worker. His father accused him of impertinence, but impertinence became audacity when Alexander successfully tamed the horse, which he did through delicate, subtle means, rather than by force or violence. Philip's reaction was gracious and marked by pride and hope for the future. Alexander's mother may be present in this story, too. Alexander's bet depended either on a willingness to be in debt to his own father for years to come – a young boy could never have possessed thirteen talents – or a confidence that his mother could (and would) satisfy the debt from her own resources. Either way, the risk was tremendous, and Alexander's actions show unshakeable confidence. From his youth on, then, Alexander's life was dedicated to facing risks, assessing them, and winning.

2

OPPORTUNITIES AND RISKS AS A TEENAGER (340S TO 338 BC)

§I.

Alexander had treated the warhorse Bucephalas as he wanted to be treated himself – by persuasion rather than compulsion. According to Plutarch, Philip knew his son could not be forced to do anything, only persuaded through reasoning. Recognizing this trait, in addition to Alexander's boundless desire for knowledge, Philip secured the most persuasive teacher he could find to educate his son to become the best possible successor to the throne of a world power: the scientist, philosopher, and political theorist Aristotle. Aristotle was the same age as Philip, born in the late 380s, and although Greek he had spent his childhood in the Macedonian court, where his father was employed as the official physician. He and Philip were most likely childhood friends. When Aristotle was about eighteen years old, he left Macedonia to study at Athens with Plato, the leading philosopher of the time and himself a student of the famously controversial Socrates. Plato's curriculum emphasized mathematics, geometry, political theory, and ethics. Aristotle became the best-educated person in Greece and, in later times, the most influential thinker from ancient Greece. During his long career, he lectured on a dazzling diversity of subjects: botany, zoology, geography, mathematics, geometry, rhetoric, political history, political philosophy, strategic policy, literary theory, metaphysics, astronomy, the meaning of dreams, and philosophy as a practical guide for living a life of excellence (*aretē*).

Philip sent Alexander and his Companions to study under this foreign teacher in a sacred location, the Sanctuary of the Nymphs in Mieza, two days' journey from the capital. The teenagers lived and studied apart from their parents and the rest of Macedonian life. Philip spared no expense in setting up this private school for his son and a select few young members of the Macedonian social elite. Philip believed that this special and high-powered education away from court, with a great teacher who uniquely combined theoretical knowledge with its practical application, would produce the best possible king and the best possible friends and advisors for him.

Alexander continued throughout his life the quest for all kinds of knowledge that he began during his time with Aristotle. Alexander used to say that he loved Aristotle more than he loved Philip because, while he was living thanks to Philip, he was living with excellence thanks to Aristotle. While studying with Aristotle, Alexander focused above all on learning the principles of how to go beyond everyone else in personal excellence. To serve this goal, Aristotle taught Alexander two notions that few people accepted even as theory and even fewer put into practice in their lives. One was that that money is not something good for its own sake, that wealth is good only when put to work for worthy goals. Alexander took this principle to heart; already as a young man he said, "What good is it if I own lots of things but accomplish nothing?" The second principle was that the fundamental goal of human life is knowledge, and so the most worthy of all goals is the pursuit of knowledge. Given that principle, Alexander learned that to question the purpose or utility of knowledge was a logical absurdity; knowledge was good in itself. One practical consequence of this lesson was Alexander's lifelong commitment to sponsoring what we would now call scientific research, on his own expeditions and through Aristotle. This principle inspired both his detailed intelligence gathering for his military expeditions and his unquenchable desire to explore the world. Above all, this principle motivated Alexander to want to collect knowledge about his personal nature and the extent of what he could accomplish.

§2.

Aristotle and his student Alexander considered "understanding"(*phronēsis*) to be the best and most powerful (*kratiston*) possession of all. For a person ambitious to rule, one necessary object of understanding was the nature of human beings and how we can and ought to live in harmony with the world around us. Aristotle taught that honor is the greatest human good in harmony with nature. A man with what Aristotle called a "great soul" should seek to gain honor throughout his life. That honor had to be won in competition with other people. A great-souled man knows that he fully deserves honor, since honor – public respect from others – is the prize of excellence, and winners deserve prizes. This man of excellence knows that he can lose his honor through any failure in competition with others. Alexander took that lesson to heart, seeing himself as that kind of great-souled man dedicated to the pursuit of honor and the reputation that it earned. He embraced the prospect of a life of competition, putting his honor (and therefore the value of his life) at stake from moment to moment in every activity and encounter.

Alexander realized to the core of his being that his honor was the prize at stake throughout this lifelong competition. He also learned from Aristotle that winning in competition was the only possible occasion for happiness. The gods could send victory and therefore happiness to human beings, but only to their favorites. If happiness did come from the gods, it came only to people who pursued study, effort, and – above all – excellence. Excellence required courage, a quality that Aristotle explained meant living with a clear-eyed understanding of danger, without becoming excessively afraid or cautious. Death was to be avoided through effort, since it brought an end to a competitive life, and to seek death as an escape from illness, poverty, or sadness was the act of a coward. But death was not to be feared, since the noblest possible outcome of a life of excellence was to die while bravely facing danger.

In teaching his adolescent male students, Aristotle emphasized his analysis of the behavior of the leading warriors in the Trojan War, as described by Homer in the *Iliad*. There, the first form of courage was "political," that is, the courage of a person operating as part of a social community, not as an isolated individual. The motivation for this first rank of courage was the personal quality of excellence. And because this excellence required functioning in a social context, it included not just the desire for something outstanding for the individual (his honor), but also carried a strong sense of shame, the desire of the individual to avoid disgrace in other people's eyes. Alexander accordingly expected extraordinary courage, not just from himself, but from everyone in his group. One time, the story goes, Alexander saw a young man from the Macedonian elite assisting at a sacrifice in which the carcass of an animal was being burned; a fiery ember landed on the youth's arm, inflicting a painful burn. The young man did not move a muscle or make a sound because if he had flinched, the sacrifice would have been ruined, according to religious rules. When Alexander realized what was happening to the young man, he greatly admired his courage, and made the sacrifice last longer to increase the trial of endurance and therefore the honor that the youth gained from such a public demonstration of courage.

The *Iliad* also served as a model of how to be a king ruling with excellence. In Greek city-states like Athens ruled by democratic governments, these lessons were irrelevant, but the world of kings and heroes that Homer described was very familiar to Alexander and his royal classmates as they read and conversed with Aristotle. Plutarch says that when Alexander and his friends engaged in a contest quoting lines of epic poetry, Alexander always picked the same one from the *Iliad*: "he is the best king, both strong (*krateros*) and a man who knows how to use a sharp-pointed spear." To be the best king in the Homeric sense, a man had to rule over his subjects in a paternal way, caring for them just as father cared for his children. The king's concern for the welfare of his people set him apart from a tyrant or a despot. Aristotle taught that to deserve rule, the king and indeed his whole royal family had to possess more excellence than anyone else in the kingdom. The subjects would then willingly accept the king's rule, and they were obligated always to obey the king. The king would be guarded by the loyalty of his friends, the admirers and recipients of the benefits of his supreme excellence. Ruling this way brought the king the personal honor that represented the most valued prize for Alexander and his peers in the competition defining their lives.

Aristotle also taught Alexander that being a ruler brought danger as well as honor. The worst danger was not physical (the risk of assassination), but moral. Asking a man to rule added an element of the beast to his nature, stoking his desire. Desire was the wild animal in human nature, perverting the mind with visions of exercising power to satisfy one's every craving. A ruler who followed these animal urges would ironically end up being like a god among human beings, someone with no equal, a total king who was himself the law without consideration of others' needs or desires. Like a god, he could if he wished provide benefits to people, but he was under no compulsion or necessity to do anything other than satisfy his own desire. If his subjects angered him, he could punish or kill them without remorse, just like a god.

Ruling by that template, however, would mean ignoring the overriding importance of *phronēsis*, which Aristotle taught demanded that a king rule over not just his subjects but most importantly over his own desire, his own urge to satisfy his personal pleasures. To possess understanding – and nothing else mattered if a man lacked that – the king had most of all to achieve a victory over himself. A king who won that battle would then put in place a political rule that suited the condition of his population. Because he excelled above everyone else, he would not create a state based on equality and governed by the citizens. With his surpassing excellence and power, he was literally incomparable and therefore by the demands of natural justice must remain in charge of everyone and everything.

§3.

Alexander's eagerness to acquire knowledge especially as it contributed to ruling showed early in his life. On one occasion when Philip was away from court, Alexander, still in his mid-teens, arranged to meet a delegation of ambassadors from the Persian Empire in place of his father. He spoke to them as equals, charming them with his courtesy and stunning them with the depth and perceptiveness of his questions about their journey, the geography of Persia, the nature of the Great King of Persia and his wars, the strength of the multi-ethnic Persian army, and its military tactics. The Persian ambassadors later commented that Alexander's curiosity and ambition outshone even his father's celebrated qualities. They clearly recognized that not only did Alexander have a boundless desire for knowledge, but also that he was intent on rivaling and exceeding his father's achievements. Alexander was known to have said to his friends, whenever his father won a victory, "My friends, my father will beat me to everything; he will leave me, and you all too, nothing great and glorious to show off to the world."

Philip was in fact winning many victories, through force and through diplomacy. In the decade of the 350s he seized lands in Thrace, northeast of Macedonia, that were rich in gold mines. These lands brought an annual income of 1,000 talents to the king's treasury (a single talent was equivalent to 20 to 25 years' wages for a working man). Just as adept at employing "soft power" as hard, Philip used this money to win allies. He would tell people that he won more friends "with gold than with iron," meaning that his money was more effective than his sword. In the next decade, Philip used his diplomatic skills (and the threat of his hard power – his military might) to intervene in a war among many Greek cities. This decade-long "Sacred War" involved, as the historian Diodorus describes, a bitter struggle for control over the shrine sacred to the god Apollo at Delphi. Philip brought an end to the brutal stalemate, winning the reward of being elected the leader of the international council overseeing the sacred site. The king also won innovative victories over strongly fortified cities in northeast Greece by mastering siege-warfare technology. Philip was an aggressive leader in these battles, fighting so close to the front that an archer standing on the walls of Methonē shot out one of his eyes with an arrow.

Diodorus

The work of the Greek historian Diodorus, writing in the first century BC, is the oldest surviving source on Alexander. He was famous for his enormous book *The Library of History,* covering the histories of Egypt, Mesopotamia, India, Scythia (central eastern Europe), Arabia, North Africa, Greece, and western Europe from the earliest times down to his own era.

Large parts of his long work survive; books 16, 17, and the opening sections of 18 offer a detailed account of the history of Philip II and Alexander, including episodes not otherwise recorded. For example, only Diodorus provides details on the confrontation between Alexander and the Thebans that exploded into the destruction of one of the most storied cities of ancient Greece. Scholars have tended to criticize Diodorus as a confused copyist with no ideas of his own, but a careful reading reveals reasoned judgments on the meaning of history and people's motives.

Philip's actions also revealed his ruthless reaction to opposition. While besieging Olynthus, an ally of Athens, Philip tried to convince the city to join him. When Olynthus rejected him, he determined to exterminate it. In 348 he bribed some citizens to betray their comrades and open the gates, capturing the place. While victorious armies regularly plundered, seized captives as slaves, and knocked down sections of the defeated city's fortification walls, Philip undertook the weeks-long, arduous process of destroying Olynthus totally. He burnt the homes, sold the entire population into slavery, and leveled the walls so utterly that archaeologists today have no precise idea of their form. This surpassing violence was in service of future diplomacy, to show others the cost of resistance.

Philip's intervention in the Sacred War and ongoing conflict with Athens were the result of his drive for security and resources, especially through controlling the Hellespont, the narrow entrance to the Black Sea. This body of water was surrounded by lands that produced large supplies of grain, the main food of antiquity; whoever controlled the naval routes in and out of the Black Sea could be sure to feed a large population and a strong army. The city of Athens had long ago grown so populous that it had to import food from that region, and so the Athenians fought hard to oppose Philip and his efforts to impose a chokehold on the Black Sea.

§4.

In 340, while Philip was away fighting for control of eastern Thrace – the region between Macedonia and the Hellespont – to try to weaken Athens, Alexander remained behind in the capital. Philip gave his son the royal seal, empowering him to act as ruler in his absence, making political, economic, and military decisions. Sixteen years old, Alexander seized the chance to act like a king. A tribe called the Maedi on the northeastern border of Macedonia rebelled, perhaps hoping to gain an advantage while an adolescent was in charge. Alexander led Macedonian troops against them, seizing their main settlement. He then imported a new population to refound the city. As his father had done elsewhere, Alexander populated his foundation with former soldiers and people of different nationalities; this "mixed population" would draw its identity only from the new city, Alexandropolis ("City of Alexander"), and its founder, Alexander. The teenager, by naming a city after himself, announced to the world that he intended to be incomparable.

Messengers kept Philip informed of what Alexander was doing, and the king must have approved of his son's skillful and ambitious actions. Philip's campaign in Thrace stalled when

Athens, with Persian support, sent an allied Greek fleet from the eastern Aegean Sea. Making a hasty treaty with Athens, Philip called for Alexander to join him in a new expedition against the Scythians in the north, near where the Danube River enters the Black Sea, to seek plunder to enrich the kingdom's war chest. Alexander learned a hard lesson in the dangerous uncertainties of war on this expedition. The Macedonians won a decisive victory against the Scythians, capturing a great hoard of treasure. But on the homeward march, another tribe, the Triballians, nearly destroyed the army in a surprise attack. Philip was badly wounded in the leg, and their booty, taken from the Scythians, was lost to this other tribe.

Unyielding in his quest to become the leader of Greece, Philip kept pressing Athens. In the summer of 338, he marched his army of Macedonians and Greek allies south and attacked the city of Elateia, an ally of Athens in the mountains between northern Greece and Macedonia. There Philip's army was like a cork trapping the Greeks in a bottle to the south. The news that came to the Athenians was that Philip intended to capture their city itself. This prospect was such a threat that that the Athenians panicked and quickly made an alliance with Thebes – the two neighboring city-states were usually bitter enemies – and their joint army marched out to fight Philip as far from the cities of Athens and Thebes as possible. The battle happened near a town called Chaeronea.

§ 5.

Philip gave an important role in the fight to his son. At this period, infantry formed up in a line of battle many men deep, but it was the front rank that met the enemy and was the most important for tactical planning. Each man in the front rank held his shield in his left hand and his thrusting spear in his right hand. Well-disciplined troops maintained their positions, spaced far enough apart so that each man's right hand was free to use his weapons. Aggressive fighting was always the best guarantee of safety. But when attacked, troops would often slide to the right, each man trying to move more of his own unshielded right side behind his neighbor's shield. In this way, an entire army could shift gradually toward the right while fighting. As an army drifted rightward, the spacing between men could get very ragged, particularly on the far left side of the line.

The goal of any army in battle was to "turn" the enemy's line. That is, they tried to move around the end of the enemy's line of battle, so they could attack the opposing soldiers from the side. Once an army had to defend itself from the front and from the side, the solid wall of shields and spears collapsed as men turned away from the line to face the new threat. Armies often stationed lightly armed, highly mobile troops at the extreme ends of their lines to help prevent such a flanking attack by the enemies.

The commander-in-chief traditionally positioned himself on his army's right. Here he could prevent the gradual right-hand drift and could command his best troops facing the left end of the enemy's battle line, its second best men. In this way, the commander-in-chief would be most likely to be able to outflank the enemy line, get a decisive tactical advantage, and win the battle. At Chaeronea, Philip took the position on the right, with Alexander stationed on the left. The Macedonian cavalry was also on the left, and scholars often assume that Alexander was on horseback leading the cavalry. Diodorus, the only ancient writer to describe Alexander's role, gives no indication whether he was mounted or on foot.

What is clear is that Alexander fought bravely and was instrumental in winning the battle. His end of the battle line attacked the strongest forces of the opposing Greeks, the 300 warriors of the Sacred Band from Thebes. These were elite, highly trained soldiers, famous for their courage and a combat ethos based on unit cohesion and the complete willingness of each soldier to die for his comrades; some said that the Theban Band consisted of pairs of lovers who fought side-by-side. The whole Theban army had been battle-tested in the long Sacred War, and the Sacred Band were the best of this veteran army.

Philip's right flank, facing the citizen-soldiers from Athens, pretended to retreat. The Athenians moved forward too quickly, allowing a gap to appear in their line between themselves and the Thebans. Alexander led the attack forward into this space, pivoting left to flank the elite force of Thebes. Other Macedonian cavalry, on the far left side, advanced forward and right. As the Athenians, realizing that their tactics had collapsed, fled up a river-valley, the Theban Sacred Band was surrounded. Most of the Greek army surrendered or fled, but the Sacred Band fought on until 254 out of 300 were killed.

For the first time in history, an outsider controlled mainland Greece. To celebrate this unprecedented win, Philip got drunk, a Macedonian tradition upon winning a battle. Lurching among the prisoners of war, he mocked the Athenians for their failure. One of the captives, Demades, an experienced speaker in the rowdy political debates of Athens, stopped the Macedonian king in his tracks by quoting lines of poetry from the *Iliad* that laid bare the difference between a king of excellent character and a buffoon. Stung by the quotation, Philip sobered up to focus on the problem of how to make his military triumph into a political victory. Since the Thebans had been allies of Macedonia when they joined Athens in opposing him, Philip saw them as traitors. He installed Macedonian soldiers as a permanent garrison in the city. With Athens, he reached a peaceful settlement: the king wanted to have on his side the most famous city of Greece as he began a bold new plan, a grand war of revenge with roots far back in Greek history. Philip planned to attack the Persian Empire in Asia. He would avenge what every Greek remembered: five generations earlier the Persians had attacked the Greek mainland, burning the temples of the gods before being beaten back by an alliance of freedom-loving Greeks.

§6.

In fact, in the early years of the Persian Wars (499 – 479 BC) the Greeks themselves had burned a temple in Persian territory. But in the memory of Greeks, the Persians were invaders, disrespectful of the gods, and eager to enslave the free people of Europe. Throughout the fourth century, Greek political figures such as the Athenian Isocrates made public calls for a crusade against Persia. Now Philip was going to do what no one had ever done before: lead an alliance of Greek military forces, with Macedonians at the head, to defeat and humble the Persians. The Persian monarch was so powerful, ruling territories so extensive, with wealth so vast, that the Greeks called him "The Great King." Philip's war would therefore be a heroic quest. When Alexander learned of his father's plans, he must have swelled with pride and ambition. He had grown up reading epic poems about the legendary Trojan War, and now his father was planning to be a real-life King Agamemnon, waging war in Asia against a daunting foe. This plan would require the valor of Achilles, the wisdom of Nestor, and the cunning of Odysseus, the heroes of myth whose exploits had been Alexander's education. Alexander knew from reading Herodotus that heirs to the Persian throne were not allowed to go to war until in their twenties; he, the Macedonian heir, would face no such restrictions. He was eighteen years old and would go to Asia to compete in this ultimate contest for excellence on a global scale. He needed only to remain on good terms with his father, his competitor for honor.

Philip could not leave Europe unless his position there was secure, for which he needed a strong alliance and recognized legitimacy. When he called the city-states of mainland Greece to a meeting, they all sent representatives, except the Spartans (who paid for their defiance when Philip took away a substantial part of their territory). During the Persian Wars, the Greeks had gathered at Corinth to plan their defense, and so Philip chose Corinth for this meeting of his offensive alliance, which he called "The Greeks." Philip was unquestionably the head of the alliance, but he arranged for "The Greeks" to elect him to leadership under the title *hegemon*, a Greek word for a commander of a voluntary federation ruled by consensus rather than compulsion. By masking the harsh reality of his position behind the language of equality and cooperation, the politically astute Macedonian king helped the Greeks avoid further shame. As allies rather than subjects, they would be less likely to cause trouble behind his back. To make doubly certain, however, Philip installed military garrisons at key locations in Greece.

As Macedonian king Philip also acted to build support and security in his homeland. But when he returned from Corinth to Pella, everything seemed to fall apart: the unity of the Macedonian elite behind their king, and the relationship of mutual respect and cooperation between Philip and his son Alexander. After Chaeronea, the soldiers started saying, "Philip is our general, but Alexander is our king." Alexander also complained to his friends that he was not given enough credit for the victory in that battle, or for the war with the Maedi. At this time, too, Philip accused his wife Olympias of being unfaithful and expelled her from his bedroom. This dishonor to Alexander's mother was dishonor to her son.

Competition Between Fathers and Sons

Philip, Alexander's father, was proud of his son's early accomplishments. By the time the boy became a teenager, however, they were rivals, in a way commonly depicted in Greek myth. In the Greek literature that Alexander loved, the structure of the universe arose from father-son rivalry. The famous eighth-century BC epic poet Hesiod described the violence-filled story of the birth of the gods: Gaia (Earth) and Ouranos (Sky) were the first divinities, sprung from Chaos (Void), and they produced a second generation of gods, among whom was a son Kronos. To prevent his children from rivaling his power, Ouranos stuffed them back into Gaia's womb. Kronos conspired with his mother, and when Ouranos next had sex with Gaia, the son cut off his father's genitals with a curved knife. Kronos then seized his father's position as ruler of the universe. Kronos married his sister Rhea, producing a third generation of gods. Kronos hated his children, swallowing each of them the moment they were born to keep them powerless. Furious at her husband, Rhea tricked him into swallowing a stone instead of her infant when Zeus was born. Zeus grew up hidden on the island of Crete. When he was strong enough, he defeated his father, confined him to everlasting imprisonment, and became king of the gods himself. For Alexander, this gruesome story revealed a cosmic truth about fathers and sons.

§7.

The conflict between father and son became a crisis after Philip arranged another marriage for himself, to Cleopatra the niece of Attalus, an aristocrat and one of Philip's generals. Philip intended this marriage to create a strong bond between the king and a commander who would spearhead the attack on Persia, but the banquet celebrating the upcoming ceremony turned into a family disaster. Alexander was present, even though his mother was in disgrace, and he taunted his father by saying, "When my mother remarries, I'll be sure to invite you to her wedding." Later that evening, the bride's uncle Attalus got drunk and loudly called for all the guests to pray for a "legitimate heir" to the Macedonian throne. This was a terrible insult to Alexander. Philip's new bride-to-be was from Macedonia, unlike Olympias from Epirus. Attalus was saying that a son born to Philip and Cleopatra would be more Macedonian than Alexander. But worse, he was saying that Alexander's talent, his deeds in war, did not earn him the right to be king after Philip. The young man who alone led an army to destroy the Maedi and who charged and defeated the Theban Sacred Band was less deserving than a baby who was not born (or even conceived) yet.

Alexander immediately shouted "You evil head!" (*kakē kephalē*). These seemingly bland words in Greek, which were in fact infused with the same fiery emotion as "You shithead!" in English, formed the insult that Alexander, like characters in the fables of Aesop that echoed in the ears of every Greek, used to express overwhelming rage. He added: "Do we seem to you to be bastards?" He then threw his drinking cup at Attalus. Philip leapt up and drew his sword to attack his own son. Just as drunk as Attalus and just as angry as Alexander, the king promptly tripped and fell to the floor, sprawling in front of the horrified guests. Alexander mocked his father, saying "This jerk who plans to take men from Europe to Asia can't even cross from one couch to another!"

In the aftermath of this catastrophe, Alexander took his mother and left Macedonia. She stayed in her native land with her brother, Alexander I, the king of Epirus. Alexander, however, moved northward to Illyria. This was shocking. Philip had to wonder what his son was doing, taking refuge with Macedonia's bitterest enemies. The young man had never remained idle and had been trained from childhood to act aggressively to shape his own world. The boy who would risk his life on a wager over an ill-tempered horse would hardly fail to seek revenge for an insult so horrible it drove him and his mother from their home. The insult denied Alexander's right to rule. The only possible revenge would be to regain that right, to win the contest of excellence in some way that no one could deny. Philip had to fear that Alexander would lead an Illyrian army in an invasion of Macedonia to seize power and restore his honor. This very real possibility – the son had already commanded an attack and founded a city in his own name – made further planning for the invasion of Asia impossible. Philip could not leave Europe while there loomed such a threat to his plans, his throne, and his life. The toxic combination of jealousy, ambition, anger, and alcohol, stirred up in the superheated crucible of Macedonian royal politics, was on the verge of destroying everything Philip had worked for.

3

THE DANGER IN
REPLACING A MURDERED
FATHER AS KING
(337 TO 335 BC)

§ 1.

A truce resolving the potential war between father and son came unexpectedly through the intervention of Demaratus, a Greek from Corinth who enjoyed a relationship of "guest-friendship" with the Macedonian royal family. That status allowed Demaratus to speak frankly to the king. Since much of the venom in the quarrel between Alexander and his father centered on their relative status in the eyes of the Macedonian elite, it took an outsider to make the peace. Demeratus reproached Philip for the disunity he had created in his own house at this critical time, when he was trying to maintain an alliance among Greeks for a high-risk invasion of Persia. Philip followed the advice and reached out to his son.

No source records the message that Philip sent to Alexander. Whatever words Philip used with his son, they tipped the balance of a difficult dilemma for Alexander: were his chances of survival, success, and honor better if he rebelled against his father with the Illyrians as allies, or if he returned to Pella and to the life-and-death competition for preeminence in the violent arena of the Macedonian court? Alexander returned home in late 337. It cannot have been a light-hearted reunion, and there is no sign that Alexander and his father ever again enjoyed a relationship of mutual esteem and confident, shared purpose.

§2.

Another crisis arose almost immediately. In 338 the Persian king Artaxerxes III had died. Persian royal politics were just as savage and unforgiving as those in Macedonia, and the death of a king inevitably generated plots, betrayals, and murder among royal sons and cousins, until one emerged strong enough to hold power. At this time, Philip's plans to attack Persia were no secret, and the Persians knew that a power struggle over the empty throne put them in no position to defend the empire against a Macedonian threat.

Pixodarus, a local ruler of Caria, a Persian province in Anatolia (today Turkey) on the western edge of the empire, acted to try to protect his own interests. He sent a letter to Philip proposing to marry his daughter to Arrhidaeus, Philip's oldest son and Alexander's half-brother. Pixodarus' offer of diplomacy through marriage was an attempt to buy life insurance, so to speak, in case the new Persian king proved weak and a large and deadly Macedonian army appeared on the borders of Pixodarus' domain in Caria. Pixodarus, ignorant of Macedonian royalty, assumed that Arrhidaeus was the best pick as a potential husband for his daughter, since, as the oldest son, Arrhidaeus presumably enjoyed the highest status and best prospects for the future. This assumption was faulty, however. Arrhidaeus suffered from some kind of diminished mental capacity – our sources are not specific – and he never played any major role in Macedonian politics, either under Philip or later under Alexander.

The details of Pixodarus' offer were based on an understandable mistake, but Olympias and her friends stirred up Alexander, telling him that this was another sign that Philip was trying to replace him as royal heir. Alexander took the bait. He wrote Pixodarus on his own, without telling Philip. He offered himself as husband for the Carian's daughter, saying that Arrhidaeus' disability made him unsuitable. For Alexander to offer a political alliance with a foreign power, without his father's knowledge, represented an enormous risk; Alexander must have felt himself to be living on a cliff edge. Pixodarus wrote back that he would be delighted to have Alexander as his son-in-law.

Someone informed Philip of these secret negotiations. The king burst in on his younger son to berate him. The focus of Philip's outrage suggests that in this affair, Alexander made an uncharacteristic miscalculation. Plutarch tells the story of the angry confrontation between father and son, and in this account Philip was not angry over Alexander's meddling in affairs of state, but over his bad judgment in a matter of honor. The son had calculated that marriage to a Persian official's daughter was a prize worth competing for. Philip accused Alexander of demeaning himself with his offer of marriage. Pixodarus might be a ruler in Caria, but Alexander should have seen him as a slave to a barbarian king, an unworthy ally and certainly an unworthy father-in-law.

No source tells us who betrayed Alexander's plan to Philip. It may have been Philotas, one of the Companions of Alexander and the son of the important Macedonian general Parmenion. Plutarch says that Philip brought Philotas with him when he accused Alexander. In the aftermath of the "Pixodarus Affair," Philip exiled several of his son's Companions – his close friends Ptolemy, Harpalus, Nearchus, and Egyrius – but allowed Philotas to remain. Philip either blamed these young men for encouraging Alexander to go behind his father's back, or was pretending to blame them, so he could have an excuse not to punish his own son. Now that Alexander was back in Pella, he would certainly play a large role as a commander during the invasion of Asia. Alexander stayed at court. But it must have been a shock to him to lose the company of his closest friends, and a greater shock to learn that one of his closest friends would commit the betrayal of informing on him. Even if his friend believed that by telling Philip he was saving Alexander from making a catastrophic mistake, Alexander would have seen this as a lack of confidence, trust, and thus a wound to his honor. Alexander was now even more isolated, exposed to even greater danger in an environment of rumor and treachery.

Olympias did not return to Philip's side or the company of her son. She stayed at her brother's court in Epirus. Outraged at being demoted to "second wife" in favor of the king's new bride, she worked to make her brother into an ally in revenge against Philip. Philip outfoxed her, showing a mastery of the diplomacy of political marriage that his son clearly lacked. He and Olympias had a daughter, Alexander's full sister, who was also named Cleopatra. Philip offered this Cleopatra as a wife to Alexander of Epirus, Olympias's brother and the young woman's uncle. The king of Epirus accepted, and so became Philip's son-in-law; he clearly calculated that cooperation with Philip outweighed any obligation toward his angry sister. This solution restored honor to the relationship between Pella and Epirus, but did nothing for the badly damaged status of Olympias or the deeply wounded pride of her son Alexander.

§3.

In 336 the whirlwind of Philip's diplomatic and military plans for the invasion of Asia were progressing at full speed, and the smoldering situation between father and son finally came to an end – with the murder of the king. This bloody conclusion rocked the already conflicted Macedonian kingdom when the crime was perpetrated at the royal wedding between Cleopatra, Philip's daughter, and Alexander I, king of Epirus. The wedding took place in the bride's homeland, in Macedonia's original capital city. This location flattered Alexander I, since he was the honored guest of the most powerful ruler outside of Persia, but it also put him in his place. Weddings usually took place at the groom's home, to show that the bride was now part of her husband's family, not he part of hers. By making Alexander I come from Epirus to Macedonia, Philip was asserting that he was not Philip's true equal but was under the Macedonian king's authority. The wedding was also to be an international event, a showcase of Macedonian glory, with a festival to honor the gods and ask their support for the impending military campaign that would take a European invasion force into Asia.

Philip had already asked for a prophecy from the oracle of Apollo at Delphi; according to the relationship of (unequal) reciprocity that Greeks assumed to exist between humans and gods, Philip had the right to expect good news from Apollo as repayment for protecting his sanctuary in the Sacred War. When Philip asked if he would defeat the Great King of Persia, the priestess responded as she always did, with a line of poetry in the style of Homer, uttered from a trancelike stupor: "The bull is wearing a garland [i.e. ready to be sacrificed]; the end is at hand; the one who will sacrifice it exists." This obscure verse was typical of oracular responses; questioners were left to decode the god's meaning for themselves. Philip optimistically concluded that "the bull" to be sacrificed was the Persian king, and that "the one who will sacrifice it" was himself, his preparations for war being almost complete. Brimming with confidence, Philip sent his highest generals from among the Macedonian elite, Attalus and Parmenion, ahead into Anatolia with an advance force, announcing that this army was coming to liberate the Greeks of Asia from their Persian oppressors. His war for revenge and glory was launched.

But before he crossed to Asia himself, Philip wanted to host a grandiose event at home. Everything was to be perfect, to show Philip's confidence in his plan to become the most famous man in the world. Alexander's presence and visible support was required, since the son's demonstrated excellence and hard-earned fame would reflect glory onto the father. An international crowd, Macedonians and Greeks, gathered to cheer the opening event, a parade into a large outdoor auditorium. The scale of this procession resembled the opening ceremonies of the modern Olympic games, but Philip's procession honored gods, not athletes. He had ordered artists to make statues representing the twelve Olympian gods, decorating them with costly ornaments to show his respect. These twelve dazzling objects led the parade, but Philip's most extraordinary statue was the thirteenth: a representation of himself in the same magnificent style.

The crowd must have been stunned. The full message that Philip was trying to communicate by adding himself to this parade of gods remained unstated, but there was no mistaking the king's supreme pride and confidence in his status as the unquestioned head of the Macedonian and Greek world. To emphasize this point, Philip entered the stadium wearing a shining white cloak and accompanied only by his son and his new son-in-law, Alexander of Macedon and Alexander of Epirus. He had no bodyguard. The hegemon of the Greeks wanted to show that he was safe in the goodwill of his close relatives and allies from Greece, with no need for a wall of spears to protect him.

Suddenly a man named Pausanias pulled a knife from under his cloak and rushed at the unguarded king. He stabbed Philip to death on the dirt of the arena, before the very eyes of the spectators gathered for what they had expected to be a joyous celebration. The assassin turned to make his escape, but he tripped on a vine and fell. In the uproar of the moment, armed Macedonians surrounded him and speared him to death on the spot. Like so many political murders since, the killing of Philip of Macedon invites speculation about motives and conspiracies. Did Pausanias act alone? Ancient authors agree that Pausanias acted out of revenge. Some time earlier, as part of a personal quarrel, the general Attalus had orchestrated a violent sexual assault on this man. Philip had known this and had tried to pacify Pausanias with a gift of money and a promotion, but the king did nothing to punish Attalus; he needed him to serve as a top commander against Persia. The humiliated Pausanias' resentment festered deeper and deeper until it exploded into a killing rage.

Modern scholars investigating this ancient murder mystery see signs of conspiracy. If revenge for rape was the motive, why did he kill Philip and not Attalus? Others had grudges against Philip, not least his "number two wife," Olympias, mother of Alexander. The age-old crime-solving question, "Who benefited?," points directly at Alexander, who not only shared his mother's grievance but also stood to become king in his father's place. Supporting this conspiracy theory is the conveniently prompt killing of Pausanias, before anyone could interrogate the assassin; the men who did that deed were all friends of Alexander. Did Alexander, urged on by his mother's fury, persuade Pausanias to do this deed? Or did Alexander perhaps simply manipulate Pausanias toward murder? Plutarch says that when Pausanias complained to Alexander about being assaulted, Alexander said only one thing to him, a quotation from Euripides' play *Medea* that spoke of murdering "the bride's father, the groom, and the bride."

No one will ever solve the mystery of the violent death of Philip II on the eve of his great expedition to Asia, even though it stands at the very center of the life of Alexander. Did the young prince conspire to kill his own father, to protect his status as heir and his path to ultimate glory? Regicide, the murder of a king, is always a terrible crime, but patricide, the murder of a father, defiled murderers (the Greeks were convinced) with a terrible pollution that made them hated by all the gods and unsuited for life in any community; their very presence inflicted a lethal contagion on those around them. The mythological Oedipus was a powerful symbol for all Greeks of the terrible consequences of patricide, as his (unintentional) crime brought a deadly plague to an entire city and left him to roam homeless and blind. Could someone polluted in this way go on to success, honor, and glory? The ancient sources never hesitate to suggest conspiracies and always love to report derogatory evidence about Alexander. But they never accuse him of killing his father.

§4.

There is no question at all about the decisive, violent action Alexander immediately took to secure his position as Philip's successor. As Macedonian royal heirs had always done, he stopped at nothing to eliminate every threat to his life and rule. As a royal son, Alexander had always known that his life was in constant danger; he always slept with a knife under his pillow. Now the knife came out. An accusation of "conspiracy in the murder of the king" was all the excuse Alexander needed to kill anyone who might stand in the way of his kingship. Among the first to die was Attalus. He had arranged the outrage that drove Pausanias to kill Philip, but his real crimes were drunkenly insulting Alexander's legitimacy at the wedding banquet for Philip and, now, his reported plotting to overthrow the new king. Alexander's agents found Attalus stationed in northwestern Anatolia with his fellow general and father-in-law Parmenion and the advance forces of the Macedonian army. When Alexander's men killed Attalus, neither Parmenion nor the soldiers made any public reaction. They were Macedonians and knew the stakes and dangers of royal successions.

Alexander's men killed Amyntas, Alexander's cousin and contemporary, the now young-adult son of Perdiccas III whom Philip had been protecting for more than twenty years. Amyntas was of royal blood, and there could be no chance that anyone would use him as a pawn in a plot to keep Philip's son off the throne. Every member of the royal family had hundreds of cousins, and that tenuous blood relationship meant nothing compared to Alexander's need for security.

The brutal reality of Macedonian politics demanded that the women allied with the new young king turn their hands to murder as well. As soon as Philip was dead, Olympias dealt with the threat (and ongoing insult to her honor) that was Philip's latest wife, Cleopatra, and her daughter, Europa. Although this child was an infant and a girl, Olympias had her killed; she then forced Cleopatra to take her own life. The sources say that Alexander was upset at these deaths, but they also say that he then moved to kill all of Cleopatra's male relatives. After the murder of possible heirs, Alexander and his mother had to worry about their grieving family seeking revenge.

No man could rule the Macedonians merely on the strength of his ancestry and the elimination of other heirs. Alexander's claim to the throne depended on recognition and approval from the Macedonian army. So, he presented himself to the soldiers as their king, promised to rule as his father had done, and added that the Macedonians no longer had to pay taxes to the royal family. The army approved, and Alexander now had the rule of the kingdom, for as long as he could keep it.

§5.

Enemies of Macedonia, to the south and north, immediately sought to destroy the new king and the territorial, economic, and political power he had inherited from his talented and vigorous father. The Greeks, Philip's "voluntary allies" for his planned crusade against Persia, immediately revolted and managed to expel at least one of Philip's Macedonian garrisons. The barbarians to the north planned openly to attack Macedonia, which they saw as an easy target under the shaky command of a flustered twenty-year-old struggling to establish himself as king.

Alexander's older advisors were familiar with his character and talents but nevertheless advised caution: abandon the alliance with the Greeks, give up the ambitious plans for an Asian war, and focus on protecting the country from the northern threat. A two-front war, they argued, was too much. Alexander rejected their advice utterly. He immediately marched the army south into Thessaly and then on to Thebes. Surprised and dismayed by his swift appearance in their own territory, the Greeks caved in, reaffirmed their alliance with Macedonia, and acknowledged his leadership in the place of his father. At a meeting in Corinth, the Greeks formally recognized Alexander as hegemon and commander-in-chief of "The Greeks."

Far from seeming overwhelmed by the challenges of disarming or destroying enemies both at home and abroad, Alexander took time during this crisis to pursue knowledge and insight into the best way to live. While in Corinth receiving honors from the chastened Greeks, Alexander paid a visit to the philosopher Diogenes. This unconventional thinker was notorious for living precisely as he pleased from moment to moment; he was homeless on purpose, often sleeping in a large overturned jar, and he conducted every aspect of his life, including defecating and masturbating, without shame in public. His critics said he lived "like a dog." (The Greek for this sneer gives us the word "cynic.") Diogenes' intention was to show his contempt for the ordinary conventions of society.

When Alexander found him, Diogenes was lying on the ground sun bathing. The newly acknowledged leader of the Greeks asked the philosopher if he wanted anything. "Well, yes," replied Diogenes, "move over. You're blocking my sun." Alexander's friends mocked the penniless and nearly naked philosopher, but the newly acknowledged leader of the Greeks said to them, "If I weren't Alexander, I would be Diogenes." Alexander's friends saw a disheveled eccentric. Alexander saw, Plutarch tells us, a man confident that he knew the best way to live and certain that he was better than other men. Alexander admired this supreme confidence because he felt precisely the same way.

§6.

Armies in the ancient Greek world generally did not conduct sustained operations in the winter, when resupply by land or sea was extremely difficult. Alexander therefore returned home for the winter of 336–335. In the spring of 335, however, he led his army north from Macedonia 300 miles to the Danube River, through rugged mountains and among hostile northern tribes. Alexander was clearly equal to the logistical challenges of land navigation and provisioning for a swift offensive war. He showed the world that he had the command ability to motivate veteran soldiers on a difficult campaign. Most spectacularly, he demonstrated that even as a newly designated, very young king dealing with the everyday challenges of leading an army on the march, he was capable of constantly devising innovative and flexible plans to fight a cunning and dangerous enemy.

Alexander marched with scouts deployed ahead and on his flanks. These gathered intelligence that a band of Thracians planned an ambush, stationing rock-laden wagons high on a mountainside with plans to roll them down on the Macedonian troops as they marched up a narrow valley. Forewarned by his scouts, Alexander briefed his men to expect the ambush. The Macedonians spread out their formation, making gaps for the wagons to pass harmlessly through. In those places where the terrain prevented a loose formation, Alexander instructed his men to form a tight cluster, stooping with shields interlocked overhead; here the Thracian wagons rolled over and past the crouching troops. Nowhere did the wagons do any harm. The ambushers were ambushed. Alexander's men routed the enemy and captured a rich haul of spoils.

Alexander proved he could innovate offensive tactics as well. The Triballians were a foe in the path of his invasion, holed up in an impregnable encampment. Alexander concealed his cavalry and heavy infantry behind a force of archers and slingers. The Triballians rushed from their stronghold to attack what appeared to be an easy target. Having lured them out, Alexander drove his heavy troops into the Triballians' flanks for a quick and decisive victory. His soldiers would have known that a direct attack on this fortress would have been costly and seen that their king's creative tactics saved their lives.

The swiftly flowing Danube River was for the Thracians like the Great Wall for the Chinese, an imposing line of defense. The river's rushing current had ruined Alexander's plans for naval support from his fleet sailing upriver from the Black Sea. Undaunted, he commandeered dugout canoes from the locals on his side of the river and had his army's leather tents remanufactured into inflatable pontoons. With this improvised flotilla, he ferried 5,000 men across in one night. Dawn revealed the Macedonians, ready for combat. Seeing how easily Alexander had defeated this "Greatest of Rivers," the barbarians holding the northern side fled, and the tribes sued for peace with this king who seemed to know no limits. In fact, Alexander's brilliance remained so vivid in memory that for half a century no Thracian attacked his homeland.

To the west of the now pacified Thracians was Macedonia's most relentless enemy, the Illyrians. Alexander marched against them next. A coalition force of barbarians caught his army in a valley where it appeared the Macedonians had no escape from a deadly crossfire. Caught between two forces, Alexander relied on what he had learned about the Illyrians while in self-exile among them not long before and devised a plan that relied both on an understanding of his enemy's psychology and on his ability to improvise new ways of fighting never tried before. To gain room for his men to maneuver, he staged an aggressive scene of precise training: his men wielded their sarissas with precision and roared out their battle cry while banging their spears against their shields. The barbarians blocking one flank retreated in awe. He then deployed his artillery catapults to provide covering fire – these had previously been used only against fortifications, never as anti-personnel weapons in the field. His archers he instructed to assume firing positions standing in the stream at his army's back. Underneath a barrage of heavy and light missiles, the Macedonian troops escaped through the water without losing a man. A few days later Alexander took his revenge and preserved his honor by secretly re-crossing the channel at night and destroying the enemy, who thought he had run away.

Arrian

Arrian, writing in Greek in the second century AD, had a successful government and military career in the Roman Empire. His experience as a commander makes him the only surviving ancient source on Alexander with direct knowledge of how an army operated. In his introduction to his account of Alexander's expedition (*The Anabasis* = *The March Up Country*), Arrian reveals that he sees himself as competing with the others who had written about Alexander. He criticizes others' works as sometimes contradictory and explains that he has relied on the (now lost) histories of Ptolemy and Aristobulus.

Arrian was immersed in Greek philosophy, especially Stoicism, and wrote a work recording the ideas of the famous Stoic teacher, Epictetus. In telling Alexander's story, Arrian makes clear that philosophically based principles are crucial to guide one's life. At one of the few places where he expresses criticism of Alexander (4.7.5), he remarks that nothing – not even physical strength or social eminence or successes in war even greater than Alexander's – is of any use for one's flourishing happiness unless the person who has accomplished great things also has thoughtful self-control, because no other victory matters if one fails to win the victory over oneself.

The historian Arrian, whose account of Alexander's career once he became king is generally regarded as the most authoritative that we have, introduces in his description of the Danube expedition a provocative interpretation of Alexander's motivation. Arrian says that "*pothos* took hold of Alexander to go beyond the Danube." *Pothos* in Greek means something like "the desire for what you don't have, a longing, a yearning." (*Pothos* should not be confused with *pathos*, "experience or suffering.") It even implies sadness at missing what you once had, or at least what you really wish you could have. What does Arrian mean by using this word to explain Alexander's motivation? Why did Alexander "long" to go beyond a river he had never seen before? Of course, as Arrian remarks, Alexander's vision of his own honor demanded that he cross the river to defeat the barbarians who were threatening him from the other side, but why then the *pothos* "to go beyond"? One possibility was that once again Alexander's reading about great figures of the past inspired him with a longing to win even greater glory than they; he would be inconsolable if he could not "go beyond" them. In this case, he would have remembered Herodotus' account of how almost 200 years earlier the famous Persian king Darius I – the Great King who sent the first Persian invasion against Greece in the Persian Wars – had "gone beyond" the Danube. But Darius' "going beyond" had ended in disgraceful failure. The northern barbarians forced him to retreat in fear back to the southern side of the river and slink home. Alexander, we can imagine, longed to surpass Darius by "going beyond" the Danube on a successful military campaign, an expedition that would establish a record of glory instead of humiliation for later generations to read about. And that is precisely what Alexander accomplished by transporting his troops across the river at great risk; the barbarians panicked when he appeared suddenly on their side of the river. Not only did they fail to chase him away with his tail between his legs as their ancestors had done to Darius, they made a peace on his terms that lasted for two generations, even though he never visited the region again. Crossing the Danube, Alexander satisfied his *pothos*: he went beyond what anyone in the world had ever done before, establishing for his reward the memory in the minds of future people, a "fame that does not die," as Homer says of what Achilles longed for. At this point Alexander had been king for one year.

§7.

Alexander knew that his northern expedition added to the eternal accounting of his glory. To the Greeks down south, however, it was invisible. No one knew what he was doing, and there were even rumors that the young upstart had been killed in Illyria; given the ferocity of the northern tribes and Alexander's youth, these rumors were easily believable. Some of the Greeks, who had been honoring Alexander as their new hegemon less than a year ago, now declared their independence from Macedonian leadership. Alexander was still far in the north, but he was better informed than the Greeks and learned of this betrayal of oaths. The city of Thebes was the ringleader in this revolt from the alliance sworn to at Corinth, and so Alexander aimed his army at that city, 450 miles away. He reached it in fourteen days, marching his men over wild and rugged terrain, across four mountain ranges, under constant threat of attack of hostile warlike tribes. An army on the march is normally like a ponderous, slow-moving snake; word of its progress speeds ahead of its stately advance. Alexander's army moved more swiftly than any report, so that "he was his own messenger to Thebes," to use an ancient Greek expression. The Greeks were as terrified by Alexander's impossibly abrupt appearance in Theban territory as the barbarians had been when he crossed the Danube, but they nevertheless refused to come to terms. What followed was a disaster for the people of Thebes and a controversial moment in Alexander's early reign.

Even though Alexander reached Thebes more swiftly than anyone thought possible, he did not rush to attack his rebellious allies. He waited two days, hoping that the Thebans would voluntarily rejoin "The Greeks." Thebes was the home of his ancestor Heracles, and it was the setting of many of the myths that had informed the literature of Alexander's childhood and youth, including that of Oedipus. Even after the Thebans sent a sortie of cavalry and lightly armed troops out from their walls to harass the Macedonian army, killing several of Alexander's soldiers, the king stayed his hand. What happened next is unclear. Arrian's account is the most straightforward: when one of Alexander's sub-commanders attacked the city without authorization, Alexander ordered a full-scale assault to protect the exposed unit. Diodorus and Plutarch tell the story differently. According to Diodorus, Alexander called on the Thebans to fulfill their obligation to "The Greeks" and return to "shared peace among partners," the formal goal of the alliance. Plutarch says that Alexander demanded that the Thebans surrender the ringleaders of the rebellion, in exchange for "forgiveness without punishment" for everyone who returned to the alliance. In reply, some of the Thebans called out from the towers of the city walls that freedom-loving Greeks should join them *and the Persian king* in destroying "the tyrant of Greece." Hearing this, Alexander felt "extreme pain" and ordered his army to attack the city.

"The tyrant of Greece" was an unforgivable insult. Alexander always viewed the present through the lens of the past, and he knew that what bridged the past, present, and future was the power of words, particularly words in literature. In all of Greek literature that survives today, the rare phrase "the tyrant of Greece" occurs most pointedly in Euripides' play *The Bacchae* (*The Worshippers of Dionysus*). Alexander loved Euripides, and he knew this play particularly well, since Euripides wrote it half a century earlier while living in Macedonia at the royal court. The play was about the nature of Dionysus, the god whom Alexander's mother favored in her private worship and whose mythical trek eastward toward India had fired

Alexander's imagination. In the play, Pentheus, king of Thebes, is called "the tyrant of Greece" for his youthful folly in rejecting the god and the freedom that Dionysus offered human beings. The Thebans knew what they were doing when they hurled this insult. Like Pentheus, Alexander was young and headstrong and considered himself the rightful master of their city. But Pentheus was a young fool; in the play he is deluded by the god, depicted – in a very disturbing scene – as dressing in women's clothing before wandering off to be torn apart, literally limb by limb, by his own mother and the other women of the city. Alexander's sense of honor led him to emulate Achilles or Heracles, and he could not stand for an instant any comparison to the passive, feckless Pentheus.

Alexander's army of Macedonians and Greeks captured Thebes. He called an assembly of representatives of his loyal Greek allies, and with their encouragement enslaved the Theban population and destroyed the city's buildings. Thebes would serve as an example of what lay in store for any who betrayed oaths of loyalty to Alexander. Setting a pattern that he would follow throughout his career, Alexander did not shrink from direct, complete, and savage retribution, but he also recognized accomplishment and courage with both symbolic and direct mercy. Amid the destruction, he ordered his men to spare the house of the famed poet Pindar and to protect the poet's descendants still living in Thebes. He also spared a Theban woman, Timocleia, who had murdered a Thracian commander in Alexander's army. This man had caught Timocleia at her house in the city and raped her. Afterwards he demanded money to spare her life. She told him that the family's fortune was hidden in a well in the courtyard; when he bent over the rim of the well, she pushed him in and hurled stones down upon him until he died. The dead commander's men dragged Timocleia before Alexander for punishment. She was fearless, proudly telling the king that her brother had fought against him and his father at Chaeronea, fighting to defend "the freedom of the Greeks." Admiring her courageous sense of her own dignity, Alexander let her go free with her children.

Turning next to Athens, Alexander demanded that it surrender the men who had led that city in rebellion. The Athenians were terrified, having seen the fate of Thebes. They sent the orator Demades to the king. This was the same man who had reproached Philip for his boasting after the battle of Chaeronea, and now he came to plead with Philip's son. Alexander had since childhood been unmoved by fear but remained open to persuasion. As Philip was persuaded to reconcile with his son by Demaratus, Alexander was persuaded by Demades' brave speech. Alexander rescinded his orders to punish the Athenians and re-established allied relations with the city that was still the cultural capital of the Greeks.

§8.

With all of Greece (except for Sparta) now lined up on his side, Alexander bent all of his energies to the invasion of the Persian Empire. Alexander had complex motives for continuing his father's plan, now delayed two years as Alexander established himself as a king and commander worthy of the name and equal to every one of Philip's ambitions. This invasion would bring glory to the man who led the united Greeks in taking revenge against the world's greatest power. Alexander would emulate, then surpass the example of the god Dionysus in exploring and conquering the distant "East." He would uncover and record knowledge about the nature and extent of the Eastern world and its peoples, who were still largely unknown to most Greeks. Through these goals and more, he would "go beyond" in demonstrating his excellence, following what he believed to be his own true and unique nature.

Alexander rejected the recommendations of his older advisors, who warned of the danger of moving too quickly. The king should wait, they argued, until he had married and fathered an heir of his own; there was no other way to ensure political stability among the Macedonians during a long, dangerous, and distant war. Alexander heatedly replied that in an enterprise that was honorable and glorious, any delay brought shame and disgrace. He was not naïve, and he had learned from his father's skill in wielding soft power, so he bought good relations among the social elite through gifts of royal land and property. When his friends, astonished at the amount of his awards, asked what would be left for the king himself, Alexander replied, "My hopes." After taking these steps to ensure good will from his countrymen, he went to great lengths – and in all sincerity – to win the favor of the gods. He hosted an international festival and athletic competition honoring Zeus and the Muses, deities of knowledge, art, and culture, and the daughters of Zeus. Plutarch tells us that Alexander also went in person to Delphi to consult the god Apollo at his shrine, but the shrine was closed. When he tried to drag the priestess to the temple so she could give him a formal message from the god, she spontaneously shouted, "You are unbeatable!" This was good enough. The priestess's words recalled the oracle's message to Philip when Alexander was born, and they reassured him that he did indeed possess divine favor for his expedition, the essential support for his drive for the excellence to "go beyond" and the reward it would bring.

THE OPENING BATTLES
AGAINST THE PERSIAN
ARMY
(334 TO 332 BC)

§ 1.

Alexander commanded a large army by Macedonian and Greek standards. As he started his expedition in 334 he had 10,000 men in his advance force already in Asia, 32,000 infantry (heavily armed phalanx-men and lightly armed, maneuverable skirmishers), and 5,000 cavalry. "The Greeks" provided significant contingents of men, and Alexander's expeditionary force probably comprised about 40 percent Macedonians, 40 percent Greeks, and 20 percent other Balkan peoples. To keep his homeland secure, Alexander left a garrison of 12,000 infantry and 1,500 cavalry under Antipater, an experienced commander of Philip's generation. Antipater was reliable. During the traditional wine-soaked dinner parties that were the mainstay of social life in Macedonia, Philip used to say, "Oh, now we really have to drink; Antipater is here to stay sober."

But compared to his enemy's forces, Alexander's army was puny. Over the 200 years of its history the Persian Empire had grown vast. Its heartland, the home of the ethnic Persians, was Iran, but its provinces extended to what is now Turkey in the west, to Afghanistan and the Indus River Valley in India and Pakistan in the east, to the steppes of the Central Asian republics in the north, and to Egypt in the south. At least thirty different peoples were subjects of Persia, administered locally by regional governors called "satraps." The imperial territory of Persia was fifty times larger than mainland Greece and Macedonia combined; its population was twenty-five times more numerous. The Great King held supreme power, ruling from great palaces in several capital cities. His subjects' duties were to pay taxes, send soldiers to his army, and remain loyal. The Macedonians were beggars compared to the Persian king. His treasuries contained mounds of gold and silver, ready to be struck into coins at royal command. His army boasted 100,000 infantry from the many peoples of the empire, but his pride was the cavalry, 20,000 strong at full muster. The Persian navy was lavishly funded and large, with the best ships and sailors furnished by the Phoenicians, a people with centuries of experience on the sea. The Great King also employed tens of thousands of Greek mercenaries as heavy infantry – the superiority of Greeks at fighting on foot was universally recognized. An army must be able to move, and toward this end, the Persian Empire was crisscrossed with an elaborate system of roads linking the major centers. Nevertheless, the distances were vast and the terrain often rough. The empire's extent, the large ethnic diversity of the huge army, and the babble of different languages of its troops created perpetual challenges of logistics and command.

Alexander faced more pressing problems. He commanded far fewer men, horses, and warships, but the worst was a shortage of ready cash. It had been expensive to gather and equip his army, feed them, and arrange for transport to Asia. When he finally crossed over the Hellespont, the strip of water separating Europe from Asia, he arrived with only 70 talents in money and 30 days' provisions for his men and animals. If he did not win early and win big, his expedition was doomed.

§2.

Alexander's opening foray into Asia was anticlimactic. An amphibious landing on a hostile shore is the riskiest undertaking in warfare. His army was at its most vulnerable disembarking from boats in a swiftly flowing channel onto a shore. This is why Philip had sent the advance force, to secure a beachhead. But the Persians offered no resistance to Alexander's crossing. It is possible that Darius III, the Great King, did not fully recognize the danger posed by this youth heading (by Persian standards) a weak force. Darius was probably also preoccupied with the years-long bloody struggle over his royal succession. He delegated the problem of dealing with the invader to Memnon, a Greek general from the island of Rhodes. Perhaps the new king did not yet feel safe entrusting a large army to a Persian commander and thus a potential rival.

Reading the Greek historian Herodotus had taught Alexander that crossing the divide between the continents of Europe and Asia was an act of such significance that the gods took notice. Bringing an army across this divide verged on hubris, the terrible crime of arrogantly and violently "getting above your station," a crime the gods took very seriously. For Alexander – always respectful of religious imperatives and historical lessons from literature – the need to placate the gods was every bit as important as the need to feed his soldiers or fortify an encampment. He took time, therefore, to act properly. Alexander crossed the Hellespont himself, separately from his main force, so that he could honor the gods and heroes at ancient Troy, the setting of the battles described in Homer's *Iliad*, just as (he also read in Herodotus) the Persian king Xerxes had done when he crossed from Asia to Europe to attack Greece 150 years earlier. On both sides of the strait, where Alexander departed Europe and landed in Asia, he built altars to Zeus, Athena, and Heracles. On his ship, in mid-crossing, he sacrificed a bull and poured a libation of wine to Poseidon and the Nereids, who ruled the sea. When he approached the shore he cast a spear into it, proclaiming that it was "spear-won, from the gods." Once at Troy, he sacrificed to Athena. He also sacrificed to Priam, the legendary (defeated) king of Troy; this sacrifice was an act of contrition, begging forgiveness because Alexander was a descendant of Neoptolemus who, epic poetry taught him, had murdered the old king when the Greeks took Troy. Finally, Alexander sacrificed to Achilles, "best of the Greeks." He wistfully remarked that Achilles was fortunate to have a friend in life, Patroclus, and in death Homer, the poet who immortalized Achilles by singing of his deeds. When Alexander received a promising omen at the temple of Athena at Troy, he was overjoyed; he took as a memento a shield that had been dedicated at the sanctuary, leaving his own armor in its place. This sacred object went before Alexander into subsequent battles, a sign that he had earned the support of the goddesses Athena and *Nikē* (the divine spirit of victory).

§3.

As Alexander moved south, his greatest obstacle was, initially, the daily challenge of finding enough food for his army – the soldiers and supporting personnel (engineers, blacksmiths, teamsters, cooks, medics, porters), and the animals (warhorses, draft horses, oxen). Darius' deputy, the Greek Memnon, advised the Persian generals to withdraw in the face of the invaders, destroying crops and stores of food along their line of retreat. This tactic of "scorched earth" would have quickly reduced Alexander's army to starvation and might very well have proved successful. The Persian commanders refused. Their sense of their own status and their jealousy of Memnon's standing with the Great King led them to choose a more direct (and in their view more honorable) course of action: forming a defensive position along the east bank of the Granicus River in northwest Anatolia. They stationed their cavalry in front of their infantry (of which the 20,000 Greek mercenaries were by far the most effective). This formation meant that the Greek infantry in the Persian army were not positioned at the top of the riverbank, where they could meet Alexander's men as they crossed the river and drive into them from higher ground with their thrusting spears.

Parmenion urged Alexander not to attack. The enemy held the higher ground across the river but would surely withdraw once they saw the full size of Alexander's forces. Why fight their way across, if they could simply wait and climb up unopposed? Alexander replied that he would attack at once; it would be a disgrace to wait. To show his own confidence and make clear to the army what was at stake, he ordered the men to consume every bit of food in their limited supply. Tomorrow, he told them, they would dine on a feast taken from their enemy.

Alexander opened the battle by leading a cavalry charge through the stream and up the bank, with his infantry following close behind. In his polished armor and white-plumed helmet he stood out, easy for his men to follow, but an inviting target for the enemy. His troops struggled at first, emerging from the water and having to fight up onto the far bank of the river. But Alexander's personal example and their own discipline drove them forward, and they used their longer spears to disrupt the front of the Persian lines. In the heat of battle, Alexander came within an inch of death when an enemy blow cut his helmet nearly in two. Alexander killed that attacker with a spear in the chest, but another Persian raised his sword to slash at Alexander's unprotected head from behind. Cleitus rode forward and slashed off this attacker's arm, a split second before he could split the skull of the king.

The Macedonians punched through the Persian cavalry, sending them into headlong flight from the field. The Greek mercenaries were surrounded before they could enter the action. Most were slaughtered where they stood. Only two thousand survived to be captured; they were sent back to Macedonia to work as agricultural slaves, a punishment for what Alexander called their betrayal of the freedom of the Greeks. The only Greeks who escaped were the few who hid among the heaps of dead bodies until they could slip away undetected. Alexander sent 300 sets of enemy armor to Athens to be given as an offering to Athena, with the inscription "Alexander, the son of Philip, and all the Greeks, except the Spartans, present this offering from the booty taken from the foreigners living in Asia." At this early stage in the war of revenge, the hegemon of "The Greeks" was still eager to declare his commitment to the alliance's shared mission of revenge.

§4.

The victory at the Granicus River led most of the Greek city-states and non-Greek regimes under Persian control along the coast of western Anatolia to come over to Alexander's side. He declared that they were now "free," but he expected them to remain loyal allies of Macedonia. Alexander was quick to reward cooperation. When the Persian governor in the area surrendered the local capital, Sardis, with its full treasury, Alexander responded by treating him as an honored guest in his camp. When Ada, the former queen of the region of Caria, offered him an alliance and asked to adopt him as her son, he readily accepted his new "mother," vivid evidence of the emotional depth that Alexander attached to ties of personal loyalty as the foundation of political power. If Alexander suspected resistance, however, he was ruthless. When he decided to punish the Greek city of Lampsacus for collaborating with the Persians, its people in a panic sent Anaximenes, a famous scholar, to beg Alexander for mercy. Before Anaximenes could speak, the king swore before the gods that he was going to do the exact opposite of whatever Anaximenes asked. The ambassador therefore immediately requested that Alexander make slaves of the city's women and children, destroy its buildings, and burn down its temples. Bound by his respect for the gods, Alexander preserved Lampsacus. Irritated but impressed by Anaximenes' audacious tactic, Alexander took him along on the expedition, and Anaximenes wrote a history of Alexander (and another one of Philip II).

Warships

The main warship in Alexander's time was the *trireme*, 120 feet long and 20 feet wide. About 170 oarsmen per ship, arranged in three banks on each side, rowed a trireme into battle. Some marines were stationed on deck. The ship was its own main weapon: combat consisted of maneuvers aimed at ramming the enemy with a metal-covered ram protruding from the bow under the waterline. Triremes were able to advance, reverse, and turn quickly. A modern reconstruction of an ancient trireme demonstrated a maximum speed of about nine miles per hour. Triremes bore a single mast mounting a square-rigged sail for travel; it was not used in battle.

Service on a trireme was uncomfortable, even squalid. The three banks of oarsmen were tightly packed, and in the terror of battle men would find themselves soiled by their comrades' vomit, urine, and excrement. Death could come to the crew at the end of a boarding party's sword or enemy arrows or by drowning after a fatal ramming of the ship.

The Greek city of Miletus and the Carian city of Halicarnassus (birthplace of the historian Herodotus) put their faith in the Persian navy, much larger than Alexander's fleet of warships supplied from various city-states. They refused to yield, but the Persian fleet failed to arrive in time. When Alexander captured Miletus, he pardoned the city. Admiring their courage (in resisting) and their loyalty (to the Persian rulers to whom they had, after all, promised allegiance), Alexander demonstrated that in policy as in tactics he was flexible and responsive to changing circumstances.

At this crucial moment, Alexander made the innovative – and risky – decision to send almost all of his warships back to their home bases in Greek cities. To this day the reasons behind this decision are unclear, but they cannot have been thoughtless. Perhaps he did not sufficiently trust his all-Greek fleet. Or perhaps it was the cost. Naval warfare was incredibly expensive; oarsmen expected pay as well as rewards after victories because they usually had no share in the plunder won on land. Or Alexander's fleet might have seemed too small to oppose the superior Persian navy. Alexander was bold in his tactics and personally fearless in battle, but sending a fleet into battles that they could not win made no sense. Certainly, his success so far suggested that he could neutralize Persian naval power and make the Aegean Sea between Europe and Asia into a "Greek lake" simply by controlling both shores, the western shore through his Greek allies and the eastern shore by conquering all the cities at the extreme edge of the Persian Empire. The greatest risk in losing his navy was the loss of rapid transport of supplies and reinforcements. Now the army was on its own, with its best prospect being to fend for itself, gathering food and wealth by advancing.

§ 5.

Protected by a high wall and a moat, Halicarnassus proved a tougher target than Miletus. Among the ancient Greeks, siege warfare was not yet a highly developed art. Walled cities usually fell through treachery, someone inside opening the gates to someone outside. Alexander once again showed his drive to go beyond the achievements of the past. Following Philip's example, he conducted a fierce, disciplined, and protracted siege, marked by constant vigilance against enemy sallies meant to break his lines and resupply the city. Eventually the Persian commanders in Halicarnassus fled, and Alexander's men seized the city proper, though its garrisons and harbor fortresses continued to resist. Alexander moved on with the main force of his army but left infantry and cavalry units behind to complete the conquest. It took a year.

The prolonged conclusion of the siege of Halicarnassus revealed a new challenge for Alexander's expedition, one born of his success: he not only had to win battles to conquer the Persian Empire, but he had to leave behind valuable resources – soldiers, officers, support personnel, and administrators – to maintain security in the army's rear. As he moved deeper into hostile regions, he would have to rule his conquests from a distance, relying on leaders he could trust. He also knew that as the war went on, he had to attend to the morale of his ordinary soldiers. They had to trust that their well-being was as important to him as wealth, glory, and power. Over the winter of this year (334 – 333), he sent home on leave to Macedonia the troops who had gotten married just before the army marched off to Asia. Arrian comments that Alexander's men loved him more for this care than for anything else.

§6.

Advancing away from the coast, Alexander marched toward Gordion, an inland strategic crossroads that he needed to control. As he marched, he secured critical locations by stationing experienced commanders in his rear. For the march inland he split his army, probably due to the difficulty of feeding and watering a large army in this region. Alexander's troops, camp followers (the crowd of merchants, repairmen, and prostitutes voluntarily accompanying the army), and thousands of pack animals consumed over a million pounds of food and water every day, all of which had to be carried or found. Even under the best conditions, the army could not carry enough provisions to last two weeks without collecting supplies. In the worst conditions, that critical window was reduced to several days. No matter what, the army could never retrace its steps and return along exactly the same route it had already taken; like a city on the move, it ate bare every region it crossed.

Alexander's main force built a new road through upland passes – clearing, excavating, leveling, and packing down mile after mile of rocky and uneven terrain – while he proceeded along the southern coast, before turning north toward Gordion. At this point, very bad news arrived concerning Alexander of Lyncestis, a Macedonian nobleman. He had commanded an advance force of the army in Thrace and was married to the daughter of Antipater, whom Alexander had left in charge of Europe. He was currently marching with the army into Asia. The king learned that this other Alexander had been in contact with the Persian king Darius. Alexander arrested the Lyncestian and kept him under guard for the time being. To kill him would risk vengeance from the man's family, aimed either at the king or his family in Macedonia, and endanger the king's support among his noble peers in Macedonia.

As Alexander marched the coastal road, walking along the beach, strong winds pushed up waves so large that they blocked his way. Just as it seemed to every observer that he would have to turn back and find another route, the wind shifted 180 degrees, pushing back the water and opening the way for the king to pass. Callisthenes, a friend of Aristotle whom Alexander had brought as the expedition's official historian, described this apparent miracle by citing Homer's description in the *Iliad* of the waves obeying the god Poseidon; Alexander's followers were beginning to see him as much more than an ordinary mortal, as was Alexander himself.

His self-image as someone greater than ordinary men motivated him toward Gordion, even apart from that city's strategic position in central Anatolia. Alexander knew from Greek literature that Gordion had been home to the legendary king Midas. Midas had come to Asia from Macedonia in a wagon, becoming king of the Gordians through the will of Zeus. He grew so wealthy that he was the first non-Greek to make rich offerings to the god Apollo at his oracle in Delphi. In Gordion, Midas placed in a sanctuary the wagon that had borne him to Asia, as a public memorial of the gods' favor. In antiquity just as today, the name "Midas" invoked the image of unimaginable wealth. Alexander knew this and the story of the "Gordian knot," the twisted binding of cords that tied together the crosspieces of the wagon's "tongue" (the T-shaped poles to which the draft animals were attached). No one had ever been able to untie the massive knot, but legend said that whoever did would become king of Asia. Moved by his *pothos*, his yearning desire, Alexander undid the Gordian knot. Some sources say he pulled a wooden pin that held the pieces of wood together, causing the knot to come apart on its own; other sources say he sliced through the maze of rope with his sword. Both accounts make the same point: Alexander solved this problem by unconventional thinking, by making his own path around a challenge that had stymied others. (The phrase "cutting the Gordian Knot" still describes taking a direct and immediately practical path to solve a complex problem.) Anyone watching Alexander at Gordion could see that he intended to rule Asia and that he would pursue this goal in the most direct way possible. When the story reached the Persian court, Darius III certainly understood. The Great King now had no choice but to leave the comfort and safety of his capital and prepare the largest possible army to face Alexander in the field.

§7.

Darius wanted to catch Alexander in a pincer movement, threatening from the front and the rear. He also needed time to assemble an army from the far corners of his vast empire. He therefore sent agents to stir up rebellion against Alexander back in Greece, and he ordered his fleet to attack Alexander's rear along the western coast of Anatolia. Supplemented by Greek mercenaries, Persian warships began regaining territories that Alexander had already conquered on his march south from Troy. Alexander was forced to spend huge sums – much of the wealth he had captured on his march – to rebuild his own fleet for defense and counterattack and to hire more soldiers for Antipater's European "home guard." Not even the death of Memnon of Rhodes, Darius' best general on the western front, stopped Persian power from its dangerous erosion of Alexander's position.

Alexander at this point faced a critical choice: to turn around with his army and deal with the threat in the west, or risk pushing on eastward to confront the Persian king before the trap snapped shut. Alexander, as always, chose the course of direct action. He pressed his advance. Did he calculate that Darius would panic and make a strategic mistake if faced with aggression? In fact, Darius did just that: the Greek mercenaries had been the key to the string of Persian victories in western Anatolia, but Darius pulled them back to the east, to join him and the forces he would use to stop Alexander's drive forward. With Persian forces now fatally weakened in the west, Alexander no longer had to look behind. He could focus on going forward, always forward, to face the Great King and win a victory that he believed would eclipse the triumphs of the most famous heroes of the past.

The Persians' last chance to block Alexander was a choke point on his route, the narrow pass known as the Cilician Gates. Darius failed to send an army to hold this position. Adopting too late the scorched earth policy that would have earlier devastated Alexander, Darius' deputy undertook to plunder the prosperous city of Tarsus in Cilicia (southeastern Anatolia). Alexander's web of agents discovered the plan, however, and Alexander personally led a mobile force of cavalry and light infantry to hold the city. His quick action saved Tarsus, with its wealth of food and treasure vital to his Macedonian army.

A revealing incident took place at Tarsus. To cool down after his intense exertion, Alexander went swimming in a cold river. He fell very ill. His regular doctors, thinking he was dying, feared being blamed for his death if they treated him. A close friend named Philip, also a doctor, stepped in and prepared a medicine for him to drink. At that very moment, a letter for Alexander arrived from his general Parmenion warning him that this Philip had been bribed by Darius to assassinate him. Without saying a word and in the presence of his Companions, Alexander handed the letter to Philip, and as the man read it with growing panic, Alexander drank down the medicine. He fell into a stupor from the strength of the drugs. To everyone's relief, the king recovered completely. He had proved beyond any doubt his reliance on – his need for – complete trust within his inner circle of friends. For Alexander, loyalty and duty defined how human beings should deal with him; resistance and betrayal were not admirable assertions of personal freedom, but dishonorable resistance to a superior power that should by natural justice be obeyed.

§8.

Alexander secured Cilicia and left it behind, secure, as his army moved further eastward. But the capture of Tarsus and Alexander's illness and recovery took time, and in this interval Darius assembled his army. The Persian king's force totaled

600,000 men (according to some ancient sources), or 300,000 (according to others), but even if it was only 75,000 as some modern scholars think, the Persian army dwarfed Alexander's. Without a vast, open and level field of battle an army of such size lost most of its advantage, and Darius initially planned to await Alexander on a plain inland from the Mediterranean coast. When Alexander did not appear, Darius moved to confront him to the northwest, as far as possible from the Persian heartland. But Alexander was moving, too, marching south along the coastal plan. The chain of hills that ran from north to south not far from the beach hid the armies from one another, and they passed by each other unknowingly. Generals have always cursed the "fog of war" that limits their knowledge of their enemy's actions, but no modern commander would dare fight under the conditions of blindness that ancient armies took for granted; Alexander's field of vision was limited to what his scouts could see, and what news his informers could bring on foot or horseback. In the rugged terrain of Anatolia, tens of thousands of men played blind man's bluff over miles and miles of arduous marching, looking for their foes and for a battlefield that would confer a decisive advantage.

They found each other in the fall of 333, with Darius to the north of Alexander, cutting him off from any retreat toward secured territory and cached supplies. But this advantage did not amount to much. Alexander had never yet retreated, and as he had shown at the Granicus, the Macedonian considered a shortage of supplies to be a compelling incentive for his men to press their attack. The armies faced each other across a narrow field at a place called Issus, pinched between the hills and the sea. The terrain was rough, with a river crossing the field. Maneuvering would be difficult, and Darius did not have room to bring his superior numbers onto the field. Nevertheless, Alexander's men knew that they were outnumbered, so to give them courage their king addressed them with a rousing speech. They were trained in freedom, he told them, while their enemies lived as "slaves" to the Persian King. He quoted the literature of Greek success, stories of Greeks outnumbered but free who battled hordes of Persians. His example was the general and philosopher Xenophon, who had written a famous book about leading a band of Greek mercenaries in fighting their way through Persian armies in central Mesopotamia a century earlier; the Greeks lacked numbers, but won through their prowess at the tactics of combined arms.

Alexander and Darius fought a battle at Issus in November. Darius sent a unit skirting the hills to outflank Alexander, but the Macedonian light-armed troops drove them away. The main battle was bloody. Alexander commanded the right end of the line of battle, as his rank demanded, and routed the Persian left with a hard cavalry charge. His heavy infantry at the center advanced with all their weight to strike the Persian center, but they had trouble making progress. Alexander saw a quagmire developing and wheeled his horsemen into the Persian flank, loosening and then tearing gaps in their lines. As the Persian formation dissolved, Darius clambered into a chariot to flee from the center of the action, and then from the battlefield altogether. When his chariot stalled on the rough ground, he cast off his royal clothing and insignia, mounted a horse, and escaped into the falling night. Alexander, suffering from a wound in his thigh, shook off the pain and rode hard after the fleeing Persian king but lost him in the darkness.

§9.

At Issus tens of thousands of Persians died. After Darius' battle line fell apart, most of the Greek mercenaries fighting for the Great King simply deserted, never to return to Persian service. Alexander captured the Persian camp, with its piles of gold and silver pitchers, plates, and ornaments, as well as the huge amount of money and valuables that Darius had stored nearby in the city of Damascus. Alexander distributed rewards among his troops, who thereby enjoyed their first, addictive taste of the riches to be won in this war against the world's wealthiest empire. When Alexander saw all the precious metal, expensive furniture, rich clothing, and tapestries in Darius' enormous personal tent, he remarked, "So, this is being a king." His words probably alluded to the fable of the peacock and the raven that he knew from Aesop, whose concise morality tales were repeated endlessly in Greek culture. The peacock, proud of its feathers, told an assembly of birds tasked with choosing a king that "being a king" meant being beautiful and prosperous. The raven then croaked, "Tell us, if you become king, what is going to happen when the eagle attacks us: are you strong enough to rescue us from his attack?" Since the peacock was commonly associated with Persia, and the eagle was the symbol of Zeus, Alexander's ancestor, the allusion was clear.

From the spoils Alexander's men brought him the one object they thought the most expensive of all, a small container elaborately made of precious materials found among Darius' personal possessions. He quizzed his friends on what they thought was the most valuable thing that he could store in this priceless piece. Receiving many different answers, he told them he was going to use Darius' container to protect the copy of Homer's *Iliad* that Aristotle had prepared. Alexander carried this book with him at all times, as the best guide to excellence in war; this copy of the epic poem, along with his knife, went to bed with him every night. There could be no clearer evidence of how thoroughly Alexander had absorbed and been shaped by his childhood education in the literature and history of the Greeks.

Alexander captured another valuable prize in the form of the royal women of Darius' family. The Persian king always traveled with his wife and family, as well as with a large harem, even on military expeditions. These women were now terrified that they would be raped and enslaved; every historical precedent told them that this was a natural and expected outcome of their plight. When Alexander treated them with the respect and honor due to royalty, they praised him as a god. The morning after the battle Alexander came to see Darius' mother, wife, and children. He brought with him his closest friend, Hephaestion. Seeing that Hephaestion was the tallest and best-looking of the Macedonians, Darius' mother mistook him for the king and lowered herself to the ground before him. When she realized her mistake, she was horrified and flung herself down before Alexander. But the king interrupted her by saying, "Think nothing of it, Mother; he, too, is Alexander." He then explained that she would be a mother in his eyes, and he treated her even more lavishly than had her biological son. He promised to take care of her grandchildren and to provide dowries for the girls' marriages. Alexander's generous and high-minded treatment of the Persian royal women greatly enhanced his honor among Macedonians, Greeks, and Persians alike.

The honor, generosity, and mercy in victory he showed the Persian royal women would profit Alexander as he continued his conquest of Persian territory. Local populations heard these stories and realized that yielding to the Macedonians need not mean poverty, enslavement, or death. His behavior put him at odds with his teacher's instructions, however. Aristotle had lectured Alexander that barbarians were slaves by nature and deserved to be treated like animals, ruled by civilized men like the Greeks. Aristotle's view came from his theory of "natural slavery," according to which some people could only be slaves because they lacked the capacity for reason that was necessary for life as a free human being. Alexander's treatment of Darius' family shows that whatever lessons he had been taught as a student, as a conqueror and policy maker he was his own man.

§10.

Both sides now had major strategic decisions to make. When the news of Darius' loss at Issus reached his forces in the west, they retreated to defensive positions, ending the pressure on Alexander from that direction. If Darius was going to defeat Alexander, he would have to meet him further east. He had to decide how he could regroup to confront the enemy under circumstances giving him a decisive advantage. Alexander for his part had two choices. He could immediately follow up his victory by punching straight through toward the Persian capital in the east, or he could move south to capture the eastern

Mediterranean coast and Egypt. Despite his eagerness for final victory and his wish for the most direct route to any goal, he chose the second option. As he explained to the army, by securing Phoenicia (the territory that is modern Lebanon, Israel, and Gaza) and Egypt, they would prevent any possibility of a Persian counter-attack against Greece. Alexander knew from his lessons with Aristotle that during the Persian Wars of earlier centuries, the Persian kings used Egypt as their base for attacks on Greece; he knew he could not risk moving farther inland without taking control of Egypt. Alexander's army, for its part, was well aware of the potential for pillage and plunder that lay along the rich coast of Phoenicia and the untold riches that waited in Egypt. Alexander had led them from victory to victory, and it cannot have been hard for them to believe that success in the south would be certain and profitable.

So Alexander proceeded down the Mediterranean coast, where he suddenly faced another pivotal choice from an unexpected quarter. A letter came to him – from Darius! Our sources give different accounts of the contents of this letter. Some say that the Persian king offered to make peace and an alliance, while blaming Philip II for unprovoked aggression against Persia. Others say that Darius offered to pay a large ransom for the safe return of his family and to surrender all of Persian territory in western Anatolia. Some sources also report that Darius' actual letter offered a ransom and vast territories, but that Alexander had an alternate version publicized – offering only peace with no concessions – in order to make the Great King seem blindly arrogant and unyielding despite his humiliating defeat at Issus. Whatever Darius' offer truly was, Alexander rejected it completely and publicly. He condemned the Persians as the guilty parties in centuries of hostility with Macedonia and Greece, blamed Darius for Philip's murder, and accused him of conspiring with Greeks to destroy himself, Alexander. The climax of his angry response was a demand that Darius either recognize him as King of Asia, by will of the gods, or compete for that title by meeting Alexander in battle. For Alexander, there was no honor to be won apart from a competition proving himself superior in excellence to everyone. Alexander's claim to the title of King of Asia showed that he intended to rule not just Persian imperial territory but in fact all of the earth and peoples contained by the idea of "Asia," a term whose limits no Greek or Macedonian yet knew.

§11.

The cities allied to Persia along the eastern Mediterranean seaboard came to terms with Alexander as he marched his army south. Then he reached Tyre, in January of 332. Built behind a fortification of walls 150 feet high, on an island a half-mile off shore, Tyre was a city famous for its cult honoring a divinity that the Greeks saw as Heracles. Alexander knew from reading Herodotus that Tyre had a sanctuary to Heracles shining with gold and emeralds that was far older than any in Greece, and he wanted to offer sacrifices to his ancestor in this famously sacred place. Alexander's abiding interest in Heracles was evident to all: the king's new coinage, struck from the riches of his conquest, bore the imprint of Heracles wearing a lion's pelt for a headdress. The Tyrians were unimpressed. When Alexander announced his wish to sacrifice in their city, they sent messengers saying that their city was closed to Macedonians and Persians alike, but the king might enjoy sacrificing at a secondary temple on the shore. They were hedging their bets, just in case the Persian king won the war.

To Alexander, the Tyrian refusal to cooperate showed contempt for his ancestors and his claims of superior merit, now backed up by an unbroken string of accomplishments against all odds. The furious king immediately made plans to besiege Tyre, enter the city, and bend it to his will. The city's location and defenses were formidable. Alexander's engineers quarried stone and harvested timber to construct a mole, an artificial isthmus connecting the island to the mainland. This would be a base for his siege engines, the largest ever seen. The Tyrians did everything they could to oppose this work, attacking his earthworks from the sea with their fleet of warships and with fire-barges rammed into the flammable wooden structures. The struggle devolved into a violent stalemate lasting seven months, but Alexander continued to push his engineers toward increasingly inventive solutions to every new challenge and setback. At last fortune favored the Macedonian king when the Phoenician admirals in the Persian navy, hearing that their homeland was now in Alexander's hands, brought their warships over to his side. This fleet, joined by ships sent from Cyprus (which also decided that its safety lay in cooperation with the seemingly unstoppable young Macedonian), allowed Alexander to attack Tyre from the water. He used these ships as platforms for battering rams and boarding gangways. His men worked from these floating siege-engines, smashed gaps in the city's walls, and pressed their amphibious attack under a rain of Tyrian missiles. The Macedonians suffered terrible casualties, but in the end Alexander himself led the charge that overwhelmed the enemy. As always with those who rejected Alexander's appeals and found themselves defeated, it was too late to repent. He punished Tyre by selling every one of its 30,000 inhabitants into slavery.

A second letter arrived from Darius. This time, the sources agree on its message. Darius offered as concessions 10,000 talents (the equivalent of 60 million day's wages for a skilled laborer), all the territory of his empire west of the Euphrates River in Mesopotamia, his own daughter's hand in marriage, and an alliance between Persia and Macedonia. Parmenion commented that, if he were Alexander, he would accept this lavish offer. Alexander answered, "So would I, if I were Parmenion." To Alexander, Darius' offer was contemptible. It suggested that the Persian king, who had turned his back on the rout of his army and fled the battlefield, was in some way equal to Alexander, who personally led his soldiers in battle after battle, paying for victories with wounds to his own body. Alexander was living the ultimate contest of excellence, and it was an insult to suggest that it could end in a draw. As far as he was concerned, the only acceptable appeal was an appeal from an inferior to a superior, without conditions. He wrote back to Darius that by virtue of his feats of arms, Persian wealth and Persian territory already belonged to him, and that he could marry Darius' daughter any time he wished. There would be no pause, no truce, and no turning back.

5

FINDING GOD IN EGYPT AND CAPTURING THE RICHES OF PERSIA (332 TO 330 BC)

§ 1.

In the autumn of 332, the Macedonian army marched southward along the coast from Tyre. All of the cities on his route surrendered without a fight, except one. Battis, the eunuch whom the Persian king had put in charge of Gaza, refused to allow Alexander to enter his city; he had stored food and hired Arabian mercenaries to withstand a siege. Alexander could easily have bypassed Gaza. The city, on a shoal off shore, posed no impediment to his progress or any serious threat from behind once he had passed. But Alexander was fiercely determined in his treatment of enemies. Those who cooperated he accepted as supporters. Those who resisted he destroyed. His view of natural justice, of the proper ordering of the world of human affairs (with himself at its pinnacle), demanded nothing less. When Parmenion told him that Gaza's lofty fortifications rendered it nearly impregnable, Alexander replied that the challenge alone required him to capture it. When Battis sent a secret assassin masquerading as a suppliant, who nearly succeeded in murdering Alexander, the city's fate was sealed. Alexander ordered his engineers to construct siege machines and personally took the leading role in their deployment. He stood so close to the enemy's walls that a catapult on the ramparts shot him with a missile that penetrated his metal armor and lodged in his shoulder. The wound bled profusely, and his friend Philip narrowly saved his life by pulling out the massive arrow. Even as he recovered from this wound, he stood at the front lines and was hit by a stone flung by an enemy's sling.

The city's defiance justified, for Alexander, a merciless punishment when finally he breached its walls. Every male defender of Gaza was killed, and every woman and child was sold as a slave. When Battis was brought before him, Alexander announced that he would be punished with torture. Had Battis pled for mercy, such an admission of inferiority might have appeased the king's sense of honor. But Battis held his tongue, and Alexander's rage increased. His men pierced Battis's ankles with cords and dragged him, still living, behind a chariot. This gruesome spectacle reenacted the scene in Homer's *Iliad* when Achilles drags the body of the fallen Trojan hero Hector around the walls of Troy. As much as any incident in Alexander's career, the siege of Gaza and the punishment of Battis reveal essential facts of the king's character. When his superiority was denied, his rage was implacable. And in his rage, he expressed himself through the dramatic vocabulary of the heroic Greek literature on which he was raised.

§2.

After Gaza, Alexander and his army overcame the last obstacle on the road to Egypt, the Sinai desert, without incident. The Egyptians welcomed him as a liberator. Only a decade earlier, the Persian king Artaxerxes III had brutally put down a rebellion in Egypt, sacking temples and even mocking Egyptian religious traditions by holding a barbecue and roasting the sacred Apis bull. This outrage was particularly shocking, the more so because it contravened the Persian tradition of religious tolerance. The Persian governor of Egypt, Mazaces, recognizing that the local population hated his government and that Darius was in no position to send aid, immediately handed over the treasury, and everything else, to the young king.

At Memphis, in the shadows of the great pyramids, an Egyptian priest crowned Alexander pharaoh, a human being elevated to the status of a living god while on the Egyptian throne. Alexander celebrated his success with a great festival, and then early in 331 he sailed down the Nile River to its western delta on the Mediterranean Sea. There, inspired by a dream that quoted lines from Homer's *Odyssey*, he instructed his architects to lay out the grid for a new city. Named after himself, this harbor city was meant to promote seaborne commerce all around the Mediterranean basin. His instincts were right. Alexandria would quickly grow to be one of the largest and most famous cities in the ancient world; its library and university would define scholarship, and its palaces and gardens would be the stage on which political dramas would shape the world for centuries.

Alexander – motivated by *pothos* according to Arrian – left the Nile to consult the god Ammon at the oasis of Siwah, far out in the western desert. For two centuries the Greeks had revered Ammon as a manifestation of Zeus; the Spartans worshipped him, as did the Athenians, and the Theban poet Pindar called Ammon "Lord of Olympus." When Alexander was at Thebes and his army was destroying every building except for Pindar's house, he would have seen a statue of Ammon that the poet dedicated in a temple. The heroes Perseus and Heracles had consulted this desert oracle of their most distant ancestor, and Alexander could not leave Egypt without at least equaling their exploits. This mission was personal, too. Heracles had faced the challenge of untangling his identity, his status as son of both a mortal and divine father, and Alexander also was driven to discover his true parentage. Was he the son of Philip, or the son of Zeus? Did he have a divine father as well as a mortal one? To ask this question of the supreme authority on the subject he had to march 200 miles across burning sands.

This desert ate armies. In the sixth century, the notorious Persian king Cambyses dispatched an army from Egyptian Thebes to cross the sands and destroy the oracle of Ammon at Siwah. His impious expedition, as Alexander knew from Herodotus, was overtaken by a sand storm and never seen again. A sandstorm also overtook Alexander and his men as they made their crossing. A miracle saved them – a flock of birds, or perhaps an escort of talking snakes, showed them the way out of the sand and to the safety of the Siwah oasis. For Alexander, this was more evidence of his "going beyond" the exploits of those famous figures preceding him.

Ancient writers give different versions of what transpired during Alexander's private session with the priests of Ammon. He wrote to his mother that he had received a "secret answer" that he would tell her when they met, but he never saw her again. A good guess is that the priests told him that he was the son of Ammon, meaning that he was Zeus's child, not merely a distant descendant. If he did receive this confirmation of a divine father, what did Alexander make of it? At this point in his life, did he think of himself as a new Heracles, a human being of divine descent who might become a god after death, if his achievements merited it? Or did he already see himself as something unprecedented in history: a human being who could become already divine even before death, in a way never before seen on earth? For the time being, he kept his thoughts to himself, so these questions remain open.

He spent six weeks on this journey to the oracle. Each week that passed was a week when Darius was gathering and strengthening his forces, as Alexander well knew. That Alexander made this journey anyway shows how much he valued hearing, and perhaps needed to hear, the god's answer to the question of who was Alexander.

§3.

When Alexander returned to the Nile, he took more time to craft arrangements for ruling Egypt, striving to institute lasting peace and prosperity for the Egyptians and thus stable revenues for his growing kingdom. As king, Alexander did not simply move from conquest to conquest, leaving broken walls and military garrisons in his wake. To ensure the longevity of his victories, he attended to the well-being of those he left behind. He had to depend on appointed officials, some from his circle of friends and advisors, but many carried over from previous administrations in the conquered territories. Some would inevitably betray his trust in the short term or the long term, and the difficulty of communication over long distances meant that he could not keep a close watch on the activities of his governors. But he did all that was possible, under the circumstances, to keep his empire cohesive.

When he returned to Tyre in mid-331, the challenge of ruling remotely over such vast territory became very clear. News reached him that his governor in Thrace had conspired with the Spartan king Agis to raise a rebellion against Macedonian authority in Greece. Agis had enrolled 8,000 mercenaries – the same Greek mercenaries who had escaped from Darius' defeated army at Issus. Antipater, Alexander's governor in Europe, had crushed the rebels that summer, with serious losses on both sides. Alexander's comment on this news shows how distant (in miles and in thought) he was from affairs back home: "Well, friends, it appears that while we have been winning victories over Darius here, there has been a battle of mice back in Arcadia." His dismissive comment was a joke, and it assumed that his listeners were as steeped in the tradition of Greek literature as Alexander was. He was joking that, if his own war with the Persian king was like the Trojan War of Homer's *Iliad*, Antipater's battle with the legendary Spartan army was like the popular parody of the *Iliad*, a poem called *The Battle of the Frogs and Mice*.

§4.

Alexander had done everything he could to secure the eastern Mediterranean and its coastline, and he was ready to march inland to the center of the Persian Empire. His goal was to confront Darius in a battle for the supremacy of Asia. Merely getting there was a tactical and logistical challenge. The route was long, arduous, and arid. Alexander's regional governor of Syria failed to assemble sufficient provisions, and the king removed him from his post. The army marched due east from the sea, not south along the easier route through the Euphrates valley, because the eastern route offered more forage. Darius had not expected this, instead anticipating a repeat of the history of Xenophon and the band of Greek mercenaries he had written about half a century earlier, an army that had marched along the Euphrates toward Babylon. Alexander knew that famous narrative, too, and he did the opposite. He ordered a forced march from Harran to the Tigris River, 215 miles in 14 days, to prevent Darius from blocking his passage across that river, a plan that had been revealed by captured Persian scouts. The Persians tried too late to implement scorched earth along the east bank of the Tigris, which would have starved Alexander's army to a halt. But Alexander's rapid advance across the river saved the stores of grain there from the Persian cavalry. The Macedonians' iron endurance on the march was essential to Alexander's campaign into the Persian heartland.

Alexander's advance drew Darius northward from Babylon, where the Persian king had assembled his massive battle force. The armies faced each other on a plain near the village of Gaugamela (today in northern Iraq). Darius had chosen this spot because it was large enough for his full contingent to deploy: cavalry, infantry, war elephants, and chariots fitted with scythes to slice up an enemy's lines. He had the ground leveled to give his cavalry, five times more numerous than Alexander's, an advantage he was sure would be decisive. When Alexander approached but did not immediately attack, Darius kept his men on high alert all night. This was a tactical mistake, as the next day saw the Persian army sleep-deprived and jangling from wracked nerves. Alexander had supplemented his army with hired mercenaries but was still greatly outnumbered. So, he devised a new tactic, stationing his cavalry and lightly armed troops outside of both ends of his main line of battle to block flanking attacks by the more numerous Persians. To support those blocking troops, he separated a formation of infantry and placed them behind his main phalanxes, ready to wheel instantly to defend attacks on the sides or from behind.

On the day of the battle, October 1, 331, Alexander slept in and arose late, a display of self-assurance for his men. They reflected their king's confidence and sent a deputation to his tent to say, "Commander, don't worry about the masses of enemy soldiers; they won't be able to stand the smell of goat that we all stink of!" The Macedonians exuded pride in their toughness, the long march on bad food, and their disdain for the Persian army in all its vastness.

The Persians attacked Alexander's center with a hundred scythed chariots but came under a devastating rain of missiles from perfectly positioned archers and slingers; the Macedonian infantry parted ranks with spectacular precision, letting the careening chariots pass through to the rear, to be surrounded and destroyed. Darius' initial gambit with his most devastating weapon amounted to nothing, and Alexander's infantry closed ranks so that the Persian center faced a solid fence of shining sarissas. Treating the battle like a game of chess, Alexander allowed the Persian left to outflank his right; seeing the opportunity they thought would assure their victory, the Persians rushed around Alexander's line, but their undisciplined enthusiasm opened a gap. Alexander sent his cavalry into the opening while ordering his prepositioned flank guard into action. Those Persians who made the turn into the rear of the Macedonian lines found themselves engaged with no exit, and Alexander's trap ground them up.

Darius, standing in his chariot at the center of his lines – the traditional position for a Great King commanding a battle – despaired and fled the field. His army was braver and served him better than he served them. They fought on and fell in great numbers, killing many of Alexander's men. Parmenion came under furious attack at the edge of the battle and called for help; the king and his Companions responded and found themselves in a fierce fight, suffering many casualties.

The Persian army failed to carry the field, but their fierce resistance to Alexander was successful in one important respect: Alexander missed his goal of killing or capturing the Persian king and thus ending any dispute over who was master of Asia.

Darius escaped northeastward from Mesopotamia, accompanied by a corps of cavalry from the Persian satrapy of Bactria (Afghanistan), some mercenaries, and Bessus, his relative and the regional governor of Bactria. After the battle, Alexander faced the strategic decision either to pursue the Great King or to consolidate his victory. He chose the latter and proceeded to central Persia to establish himself as the new ruler of the empire and seize control of the Great King's legendary treasuries. He therefore marched south to Babylon, where the governor Mazaeus handed over the ancient Mesopotamian city without a fight. Alexander's response marked a significant turning point in his strategy of conquest and rule: he told the Persian imperial official to retain his position and power.

§ 5.

From now on, Alexander behaved not as a foreign invader seeking plunder but as a legitimate successor on the throne of the Persian Empire. Those Persians who cooperated he reappointed. He also appointed Greeks and Macedonians to fill vacant offices, or to serve beside Persians. Alexander's attitude in matters of honor, courage, and war was visceral, inspired and defined by epic poetry and a spirit of competition that saw even gods as rivals. His attitude toward government was pragmatic. Homer's heroes sacked Troy and went home; Alexander left the field of battle and began to administrate. He lacked the manpower to manage numerous far-flung territories without relying on locals, even those who had previously been in service to the Persian king, and he recognized that barbarians as well as Macedonians and Greeks could demonstrate personal excellence. Assessing the ongoing loyalty of those he appointed was tricky, the more so once he had marched away, but there simply was no easy way to monitor their actions. Alexander's policies, then, reflected not only the limited supply of suitable professionals, but also a philosophy of empire, one that recognized the need to establish a multi-ethnic government, very much as he had done years before as a teenager when he settled a "mixed population" in Alexandropolis back in Thrace.

His Macedonian and Greek army did not yet fully grasp the implications of Alexander's new policy, how it would change their status from "conquerors" to something more like "colleagues" or even "countrymen." In any case, the army received six months' wages in a lump sum, paid out of the treasuries in Babylon. The month-long party that followed, fueled by ready cash and the flush of victory, pushed political reflection far away for the celebrating troops. Alexander, always looking ahead, reorganized his infantry and cavalry units to give him greater tactical mobility for the campaign ahead. His road pointed east. Master of all the wealth of Babylon, he had no thought of going home, only forward.

§6.

This wealth came just at the right moment. Back in Europe the Greek rebellion burned on, and Antipater had prevailed for the time being only by fighting a battle that cost 3,500 Macedonian lives. The king sent home a defensive fund of 3,000 talents. He also paid for the 6,000 infantry and 500 cavalry that Antipater had sent as reinforcements to replace casualties in Asia, troops that as governor in Greece he could hardly spare. Once Alexander marched from Babylon toward Susa (in present-day Iran), a twenty-day journey, he entered an entirely hostile environment. Susa was Persia, and its inhabitants were looking for no liberator and would provide no help to a foreign army on the march. His scouts had to ride ahead, searching for supplies that could be seized by force from hostile villages; he had to split his column into two, sending them by different routes, so they could forage independently. Never had Alexander's skills in logistics been put to a greater test. His army made the march and regrouped at Susa, and the king's care paid off. Susa's wealth was his.

He had begun this war following his father's plans, seeking revenge for Persian aggression long ago. He did not forget that historical justification, and from the palaces of Susa he reclaimed and sent to Athens two statues. These were of the famous "tyrant slayers," Harmodius and Aristogeiton, whom the Athenians honored for restoring freedom to their city in the sixth century. Xerxes had carried the statues away when he sacked Athens in 480. Alexander was acutely aware of the power of symbols, and he knew that historical symbols shaped meaning in the present. He remembered with a keen resentment how the Thebans had demeaned him as "the tyrant of Greece." With this gift of "The Tyrant Slayers" restored to democratic Athens from the halls of the Persian king, Alexander declared himself to be no tyrant – a leader who, by the Greek definition of the term, did not deserve to rule – but the leader of free Greeks, Macedonians, Persians, and everyone else, enjoying a superior status earned through his incomparable excellence.

Alexander continued to show, very publicly, that he was committed to a cultural understanding that included the Persians, or at least those Persians who treated him with respect. While at Susa, he received from home a shipment of clothes and fabric dyed purple, the color of royalty. Perhaps this was a gift from his mother who certainly had reason to be proud of her son, new ruler of an empire and lately proclaimed a god on earth, at least in Egypt. Alexander sent these royal trappings to Darius' mother, who had been under his protection since she was captured at Issus. The king presented them as a gift to honor his "second mother," along with a message saying that she and her granddaughters could make clothing from the fabric, assuming she liked it, and that he was sending some women to teach them how. The former queen broke down in tears of shame at this, for to a Persian woman of her standing it was disgraceful to labor like a common seamstress. From the historian Curtius we hear the next part of the story: when Alexander heard that she was upset, he immediately came to her in person and said, "Mother, the clothes I am wearing today were gifts from my sisters, who made them. I made a mistake based on our customs. Please don't be upset at my ignorance of yours. I have, I think, done my best to operate according to what I have found out about your ways of life. I know that by Persian custom it is not allowed for a son to sit down in his mother's presence unless she gives permission, so I have always stayed on my feet until you told me to sit. Many times you have been ready to throw yourself on the ground in front of me, but I have forbidden that. And the title that is owed to my beloved mother Olympias I give to you!" When, soon thereafter, Darius' mother begged him to spare a local people that had initially resisted him, he granted her request.

Curtius

Quintus Curtius Rufus wrote his history of Alexander in Latin probably in the first century AD. Of the text's total of ten chapters, the first two have not survived, and large portions of other chapters are also lost. He evidently had a career as a successful scholar and high-ranking Roman imperial official.

Curtius probably based his work on the (now lost) history of Cleitarchus, who apparently wrote an entertaining narrative focused on what he saw as Alexander's weaknesses and failings. Curtius similarly enlivens his narrative with emotional speeches delivered at tense moments and expresses pointed criticism of Alexander. In short, Curtius presented Alexander as a man of great qualities and accomplishments (see, for example, 3.12.18–20, 10.5.26–36) corrupted by his success and spiraling down into excessive anger, a pretense to divinity, and respect for barbarians (an attitude detested by Curtius).

Alexander's invasion of Asia was a journey of discovery as well as one of conquest, and the farther he got from the familiar world of the Mediterranean Sea, the more he entered a world that no one had ever seen, because Alexander was creating it day by day. His creation was informed by the power of history and literature, but reflective of his need to be King of Asia, not merely of the Macedonians in Asia. He knew from his text of Herodotus that every nation – Greeks and non-Greeks alike – believed their own customs to be the best and resisted adopting customs of others. Alexander's determination to mix customs and practices according to his perception and wisdom was a distinctive way in which he sought to distinguish himself.

§7.

Even as he tried to invent a new culture to support his goals, Alexander attended to strategy and tactics. The immediate strategic imperative was to secure the royal treasury in the capital city, Persepolis, the very heart of the Persian Empire, before Darius' agents could haul away its riches to prop up the former Great King's efforts to salvage his throne. The tactical challenge was getting there. The most direct route from Susa to Persepolis was arduous, a path through the high, narrow pass called the "Persian Gates." Even Alexander's gift for improvised logistics on the march were not sufficient for him to bring his whole army along this road, or even a majority of his force. So, taking a small, mobile contingent, only as many as the wild mountains could feed, he tried to force the pass, which was defended by 25,000 Persian troops loyal to Darius. These rolled boulders down from the towering heights and did what no Persian army had yet done: they forced Alexander to turn back. He was enraged. But he was ever the brilliant tactician and the student of history. In 480 BC, the Persian army under Xerxes came to a narrow and defended pass in its march through Greece toward Athens. Following Herodotus' account of Xerxes at the "Hot Gates" (*Thermopylae* in Greek), Alexander flanked these Persian Gates. He found a bilingual Persian in his camp who knew the local terrain, and after interrogating him he sent a squad along a precipitous path to the defenders' rear. Attacking the Persians from two sides, his army fought through the mountains and down toward Persepolis (*Pārsa* in Persian), the city named for the Greek hero Perses, son of Zeus, who (Alexander knew from Herodotus and Plato) had been the founder of the family of Darius. This heritage of course made Greeks and Persians kinsmen, as Xerxes himself had said.

Reports that the local population was working to remove the contents of the treasury increased Alexander's sense of urgency, but the terrain was hard and the population was hostile. Alexander's lingering rage at his setbacks was fanned by a horrifying spectacle. As Curtius describes it, the Macedonians were met by a pitiful group of 4,000 Greeks "whose fate has few examples in our memory." These were former prisoners captured by the Persians. Their captors had mutilated them, cutting off the feet of some, the hands and ears of others, and branding them all with hot irons. Their torturers kept them on public display to mock and humiliate these foreigners, releasing them only as Alexander's army approached. Seeing these victims of imperial cruelty brought Alexander to tears. He promised to send them all back to Greece, with generous stipends so they could make a new start, or live out their damaged lives in comfort. But from shame at their disfigurement, they asked to be resettled where they were. Alexander granted this wish, endowing a fund for their support.

Boiling with anger, Alexander reached Persepolis, entered the city, and allowed his men to plunder it violently. They terrorized the inhabitants and stole as much loot as they could. In their frenzy for the gold, silver, and other valuables at hand, the soldiers even killed their prisoners, although prisoners were worth a fortune either in ransom or in profit from the slave markets. In despair and terror, the people of Persepolis began locking themselves in and burning their own homes down on their heads and those of their own families. At length Alexander ordered his men to leave the women unmolested and with their clothing intact.

§8.

The true prize of Persepolis was not the wealth of the private citizens ripped from houses by common soldiers, but the king's treasury, bursting with 120,000 talents of silver and gold. As Curtius marvels, this sum of money was almost beyond belief. Combined with the spoils Alexander had already collected from Persian royal hoards, this latest capture brought the king's income from his Asian expedition to the unimaginable total of 200,000 talents. It is difficult to calculate an accurate modern equivalent to this sum, since we lack precise information on wages and prices at the time. If we imagine that a normal annual wage for a skilled worker today is $50,000, and that a Greek talent was the equivalent of 6,000 days' wages for a skilled worker, then the total Alexander had won through his conquests comes to 1.6 trillion dollars. Money would never again be an object hindering his drive to prove himself King of Asia and to achieve a level of excellence no human being had ever imagined.

The Persian kings had stored their reserves of precious metals either as bullion or objects, but Alexander did something quite different with the windfall he had seized so far. He established a series of currency mints, distributed across his empire from Macedonia to Mesopotamia, and ordered them to create ("strike") massive numbers of coins, silver and gold, to be put into circulation. The precise dates when these coins began to be struck is not known, but they became by far the greatest influx of coined money in history thus far. Over time Alexander's coinage transformed the traditions of economic exchange in southwestern and central Asia. Previously, almost no people had used coins except in areas populated by Greeks, or where Greeks did business. Most of the Persian Empire had relied on other forms of exchange such as barter (a mutually agreed upon exchange of goods) or bullion weighed on a scale (as opposed to coins, whose weight and purity were regulated). Now Alexander's coins flooded the entire region. They were minted on the prevailing international standard of weight, that of the famous silver coins of Athens. These were called "owls" after the image they bore of the bird sacred to the goddess Athena. They had been the only coins widely accepted in international commerce throughout the Greek world. The weight and purity of silver and gold coins mattered a great deal because the coins' face value depended mostly on the intrinsic value of the precious metal from which they were minted. Alexander's coins, like those of Athens, were produced at the highest level of quality and consistency, and the confidence that they inspired led to their becoming the standard international currency in the eastern Mediterranean world. Like other Greek coinages, Alexander's coins carried images on the front and back along with his name in Greek letters. These designs expressed Alexander's personal connection to the divine powers to which he felt closest: Zeus, Heracles, Athena, and Nikē. These gods were the ones for whom he had erected altars on both sides of the Hellespont strait, when he first crossed over from Europe on his quest for greatness. By having their images stamped on his coins, alongside his own name, Alexander delivered a message to the millions of people who handled these coins: he had a special status as the gods' favorite in the world.

Alexander did not let his newfound wealth sit idle. His ongoing war incurred innumerable expenses and would continue to do so – Darius was still at large, after all – but neither did he dedicate his treasury entirely to military purposes. He turned his economic power toward the service of knowledge, whose pursuit was for him a central function of a well-lived life. He sent fifty talents of Persian silver to the philosopher Xenocrates back in Greece, inviting him to join the expedition and commissioning from him a book of guidelines for kingship. Xenocrates declined the invitation to journey to Asia, however, preferring his new position as the head of the school that Plato had founded in Athens. He did write a book on kingship, which unfortunately has not survived, for which he kept 1 percent of Alexander's gift as payment, returning the rest. Alexander sent 800 talents to Aristotle, which might be the largest single educational research grant in history. The king's old teacher was to use this lavish funding to hire a vast group of investigators, who would travel widely collecting data from people with firsthand knowledge of animals of all kinds, in diverse regions and climates. Alexander did not finance this investigation in order to generate immediate benefits; biological taxonomy and animal behavior studies would not help the army capture or kill Darius, and would not breach a single city wall. Alexander spent this money because he believed in the value of knowledge for its own sake, the ideal that his teacher had instilled in him. He spent the money because no one else in the world could or would do what he could do and did.

§9.

Most of our sources report an event that occurred in early 330 while Alexander was celebrating his victory at Persepolis, an event that caused him great remorse and marred the reputation for excellence that he craved so deeply. The Persian capital was the site of a vast complex of elaborately decorated royal buildings known today as "the Palace." This famous architectural monument was nearly destroyed by a fire for which Alexander was personally responsible. Arrian says that Alexander ordered the fire set as a matter of considered policy, to fulfill his pledge to the Greeks that he would avenge the Persians' burning of Greek temples in 480. Other sources say that the fire started during an out-of-control drinking party, when a woman named Thais, a professional entertainer from Athens, persuaded a horribly intoxicated Alexander that he could increase his reputation with the Greeks if he burned down this symbol of Persian pride. Stumbling along in a drunken parade, shouting that they were honoring Dionysus, the god of wine, the partygoers followed Alexander's lead in holding torches to the tapestries and wooden beams of the palace. The walls and columns were carved from stone, but the heat from the conflagration of the buildings' flammable interiors was so great that cracks spread throughout the blocks. The damage to the complex was catastrophic.

"Why?" is a difficult question. If Alexander set the fire by a considered command, he was ignoring the advice of Parmenion, who pointed out that he would be destroying his own property and that he would be showing that he had no intention of ruling over Asia, only of moving from one battlefield to the next. It would not be the first time Alexander ignored Parmenion, and Alexander did take his pledges seriously. On the other hand, the sources that describe the drunken party say that the king awoke the next morning with a pounding hangover and immediately regretted the drunken destruction as a shameful act.

It is hard to make sense of this infamous episode. Alexander had kept cooperative Persian officials in their jobs as administrators of the empire, and he had treated the Persian royal women as members of his own family. All this suggests a vision that was not looking back west, but was fixed to the east. His remarks about events in European Greece – the "battle of mice" remark about the Spartans' vicious and costly war against Antipater – suggest that Alexander now considered Greek politics relatively trivial. His actions point to a desire to be seen by all as a legitimate King of Asia, rather than King of the Macedonians and hegemon of the Greeks, or even for that matter as yet another Great King of Persia, a successor to (and thus implicitly somehow the equal of) Darius. The hegemon of the Greeks might burn down the palace of Persepolis, but the King of Asia would gain nothing from such wanton destruction. Perhaps the most plausible explanation is this: the fire was kindled by a toxic combination of too much anger, too much giddy exuberance, and too much wine, at just the wrong time.

Persepolis

Persepolis (Greek for "City of Persia") was one of the capitals of the Persian Empire. It boasted grand structures that the Great King used to receive ambassadors or petitioners and to hold enormous festivals. Construction on the complex known as the "Palace" began in the late sixth century and continued for the next 200 years until Alexander captured the city. The palace extended over a terrace covering more than 1 million square feet cut out of the side of a hill and built up to create a level platform for buildings. A cistern stored water, while sewage tunnels carved under the surface provided drainage. Broad stairs provided access to the terrace, entered through a gateway hall flanked with stone statues of giant bulls with the heads of bearded men. Sculpted stone panels depicted soldiers from the elite unit of the Persian army called "The Immortals" that served as the Great King's personal guard.

The terrace held numerous high-ceiling halls, filled with tall columns of wood and stone, such as the "Hall of a Hundred Columns." At nearly 250 feet on a side, it seemed like a spectacular forest under a soaring roof. The largest building was the Apadana, whose enormous central hall, with its columns standing sixty feet high, gave the king a space to receive dignitaries that expressed his grandeur and superiority over everyone else in the world.

§ 10.

Aristotle had warned about the dangers of this kind of excess. Alexander, like other elite Macedonian men, was quick to anger at even a hint of dishonor. The timing of the fire is unclear from the sources, but most scholars put it well after Alexander's initial entry into the city, following a month-long expedition into the surrounding countryside to "pacify" (with great violence) the local Persian settlements. Having made complete his victory over Persepolis, Alexander paused to organize celebrations and sacrifices to commemorate his accomplishments. Even amid the festivities and the flush of success, it seems likely that Alexander, who had a long memory for insults, was still angry from being blocked at the Persian Gates, which he took as a personal failure, from seeing the grim column of mutilated and dishonored Greeks that had made him weep, and from the intransigence of the population even after he had taken Persepolis.

Some modern writers have described Alexander as an alcoholic whose life and decisions were determined by an addiction to drinking, but this is anachronistic thinking. Alcohol's effect on the human brain is a matter of chemistry, of course, and was therefore certainly the same for Alexander as for young men living in this century. But alcohol does not now and did not then act on a human life independently of other factors. Any modern understanding of alcohol abuse assumes a life of plenty in a technologically advanced society, and in the case of the developed world, a relatively peaceful and largely sedentary life in the context of a particular familial and social setting. Modern assumptions also assume limitless access to wine, thanks to the miracle of modern commercial food production and distribution. To understand Alexander, we have to shed most of those assumptions. He and his Companions were men who could as a matter of course walk thousands of miles, day after day, through the roughest terrain in the world, who trained for hand-to-hand combat with heavy weapons constantly, who regularly fought face-to-face with armed enemies and killed them amid a welter of blood; these men existed for long periods on rations that would starve an American athlete, and after their childhoods moved in circles that were for long stretches almost exclusively male, except for servants, slaves, and prostitutes. What any modern counselor would call "problem drinking," both in terms of quantity and social outcome, was an expected and indeed celebrated function of life in the warlike royal court of the king. Whatever role drinking played in their lives must be understood in the whole context of their lives.

Ancient thinking, informed by ancient culture, offers straightforward words that help us understand the drunken, chaotic parties that occupied many of the evenings of Alexander's life. Macedonian tradition demanded a wine-drenched celebration on the occasion of seizing the Persian treasury intact. As did his father after the victory at Chaeronea, Alexander saw getting drunk with his friends as the inevitable and necessary capstone to unprecedented success in the field. Modern scholarly studies of the patterns of drinking in diverse cultures reveal that it is commonly a standard and esteemed procedure for men, in particular, to drink heavily, even to the point of total inebriation, when the occasion and cultural standards require it. This was certainly true in ancient Persian culture, as Alexander knew well from reading Herodotus. When Persian men faced important decisions, they held meetings where they got drunk and discussed the issue; they then discussed the issue again when they were sober. If their conclusions under both circumstances were the same, then they were confident that they were correct. It was certainly the case among ancient Macedonian men that group drunkenness was a regular and expected custom with specific social functions.

This is not to say that drunkenness could not then be dangerous. Aristotle, working from a fourth-century perspective familiar with Macedonian and Greek culture, described the problems like this: drunkenness and anger are similar in impairing people's judgment. Both anger and alcohol put people in the position where, paradoxically, they have knowledge that moves them to act but also lack the wisdom needed to act well. Being both drunk and angry at the same time, the teacher explained, multiplies this crippling effect. Drunk and angry, Alexander could have ordered the palace burnt. Aristotle added, however, that being drunk in no way relieved one of responsibility for one's actions, since getting drunk was a voluntary action. It was fitting, he concluded, that the legal penalty for a crime was doubled if the offense was committed while drunk. Remorse was the only appropriate response.

As at the banquet back in Macedonia, when an enraged and intoxicated Philip had attacked his own son with a sword, so too at Persepolis anger and alcohol were the enemy of the excellence appropriate for a philosophically guided king. Alexander was exceptional, but his whole life, from youth, had habituated him and everyone around him to embracing a quick temper in matters of honor and a bottomless appetite for wine as a social bond at special occasions. Habits learned while young can be impossible to unlearn. The persistence of habits learned in youth was a human truth that Aristotle warned about in his teaching on ethics, a harsh reality whose consequences even Alexander himself could not escape.

6

WINNING THE WORLD AS KING OF ASIA (330 TO 329 BC)

§1.

By early 330 Alexander had sent the Great King of Persia fleeing to the northern corner of his empire. Alexander was master of Egypt and held the Persian capital Persepolis. The treasuries of the empire were his, and his innovative policies of economic reform, (limited) cultural integration, and political stability were going into effect over millions of square miles. The Greeks were avenged many times over for whatever injuries the Persians had inflicted in previous centuries. Alexander's body bore many scars from battlefield surgery to treat missile wounds, and his men were veterans of an unbroken string of victories against fortified cities and armies that invariably outnumbered them. Alexander could have declared victory and settled down to rest and govern amid wealth and comfort, enjoying a well-earned and universally acknowledged reputation as the greatest victor the world had ever seen, a status that his world respected and lauded (as has, for that matter, every other age in human history).

Battlefield Surgery

Doctors performed bloody operations in emergency battlefield conditions to try to save soldiers' lives; missiles caused the deepest wounds and the most painful operations, as Celsus describes (*On Medicine* 7.5). Extracting arrows was excruciating if the point at the end of the shaft lodged in a bone. Given that arrowheads often had pointed barbs, pulling an arrow backward out of a wound tore muscle and blood vessels. Therefore, it could be less dangerous to push the arrow all the way through and out the other side. Surgeons used a Y-shaped metal instrument to spread the edges of the wound to make the push or pull easier. If the arrow had to be pulled out backward, then the surgeon could use an instrument called the "spoon of Diocles" after its inventor. This was a smooth metal piece with a small hole at the front end to snag the tip of the arrow and then pull it backward; the sides were turned inward to protect surrounding flesh as the arrow was extracted. If the arrow tip was stuck in a bone, then the doctor could place small reeds around the shaft to smooth its exit and drill holes in the bone around the impact point, to prevent splintering of the bone, which made healing especially difficult. How the patients withstood what must have been the agonizing pain and blood loss of these operations is hard to imagine. If they survived the operation, then infection became a dangerous hazard. It is remarkable that Alexander lived despite often being seriously wounded. Plutarch lists eleven separate injuries that he suffered from arrows, swords, clubs, and rocks (*Moralia* 327 A-B = *On the Fortune of Alexander*).

Leisure and inactivity as enjoyed by ordinary mortals attracted Alexander not in the least. During the spring of that year he sent forth his agents to learn what Darius was doing 500 miles to the north in the imperial summertime capital of Ecbatana. These spies reported that Darius and his relative Bessus, satrap of Bactria, had managed to assemble an army of 9,000 (6,000 infantry and 3,000 cavalry), and the sum of 7,000 talents. Although a pitiful shadow of the international hoards and limitless treasure formerly at the disposal of the

Persian king, the number of men was too large for a mere body-guard, and the sum of money was too large for mere maintenance. Alexander knew that Darius intended to face him in battle again, and he acted swiftly to prepare his army to march out of Persepolis. Whatever he might have been planning if Darius had offered himself in surrender or conveniently disappeared, Alexander now had no choice but to finish this war on the field. While there was no evidence that Darius offered a tremendous threat – he had already gone down in defeat twice when in his full strength – a resurgent would-be Great King with a substantial army based in the eastern satrapies would be an obnoxious hindrance to Alexander's plans. Not satisfied with being King of the Macedonians, hegemon of the Greeks, Pharaoh of Egypt, and King of Asia, Alexander intended to march to India, emulating and surpassing the legendary journeys of Dionysus and Heracles. Any barrier to his ambitions was intolerable. And so the Macedonians prepared to march to the fight.

§ 2.

When Darius heard that Alexander was in pursuit, he led his forces off to the northeast toward Bactria. Alexander divided his army into smaller units that could be self-sufficient on the road, planning to reassemble his full force before facing the enemy. The Macedonians' marches were marvels of planning, speed, and endurance over hundreds of miles. Among the everyday miracles of military logistics that Alexander executed was Parmenion's transport of 7,000 tons of gold and silver from Persepolis to Ecbatana; this journey required 20,000 mules and 5,000 camels. In single file these animals took up a line more than fifty miles long. Even when the caravan found a road wide enough for ten animals to walk abreast, the column extended seven or eight miles from its head to its tail and took half a day to advance just its own length. Alexander himself rushed ahead and reached Ecbatana only five days after Darius had moved out.

The meaning and purpose of Alexander's war had now fundamentally changed. He was no longer fighting as hegemon of the Greeks, but as the self-proclaimed King of Asia, and fighting not for plunder or revenge, but to create a new world for himself to rule. This world was beyond anything his Macedonian and Greek troops could have imagined when they set out. The Macedonians owed him loyalty as their inherited and acknowledged king, but the Greeks were bound only by the oaths they had sworn back in Corinth, promises that they had now fulfilled. With all this in mind, Alexander released the Greeks from his service with thanks and generous bonuses to speed them on their return. Many of these, however, chose to re-enlist as mercenaries, more than happy to march off into the unknown following their charismatic, brilliant, and financially generous leader. Alexander was not the only one whose nostalgia for home had faded as new vistas appeared.

Leaving behind Parmenion, who was now nearly seventy years old and would serve well as a regional administrator, Alexander pursued Darius with a series of marches at high speed, over long distances. As the Macedonians approached, Bessus reconsidered his allegiance to his king, turned traitor to his master, and had Darius arrested. When Alexander learned of this, he doubled his efforts, rushing in a furious dash with his cavalry, 250 miles of desert in seven days. Only sixty of his men could keep up with their king. They found Darius a corpse. The Persian's former subordinates had murdered him and crowned his relative Bessus as king; Bessus had ridden off to Bactria with his newly claimed title to organize his military resistance from the refuge of the Bactrian mountains. Alexander paused to honor Darius. Whatever message of anger or revenge he had intended to communicate through pillage and fire in Persepolis, he now set aside as he dealt with his old foe. Alexander returned Darius' body to Persepolis, for burial in state in the ancestral tombs of the Persian kings. The dead king's brother was honored with the title of Companion to Alexander, the only Persian ever granted this distinction. Darius' life ended in squalor and betrayal, but to Alexander he was a legitimate king whose status demanded dignified treatment. Alexander could not imagine or accept a world that failed to display the proper respect for authority and superiority.

§3.

Bessus probably calculated that Alexander would turn southeast toward the pleasures of the warmer and richer lands of Pakistan and India instead of pursuing him into the stark wilds of Afghanistan, thereby giving the traitorous rebel time to gather forces to resist the Macedonian. Or perhaps Bessus was hoping that Alexander would ignore him entirely, hidden away in his Bactrian strongholds. The Persian misjudged his opponent badly. With characteristically thorough planning, Alexander divided his army into two sections, secured the countryside south of the Caspian Sea that would be behind him, and moved on Bactria. The Persian satraps in the area now recognized that Alexander was unstoppable and voluntarily surrendered to him. He accepted their submission and, in keeping with his policy as King of Asia, sent most of them back to their offices to serve, he expected, as loyal subordinates to a politically legitimate ruler.

One of these Persians, Nabarzanes, had been with Bessus when Darius was murdered. Despite being implicated in treachery and regicide, Nabarzanes escaped punishment. Even when feeling righteous anger Alexander had always been willing to forgive those who either expressed remorse and gave evidence that they would remain loyal, or who showed particular dignity and appropriate respect when brought before the king. Nabarzanes escaped punishment, not least because he had an advocate, a young, handsome eunuch named Bagoas. Curtius tells us that Bagoas had been one of Darius' companions, and that Darius had a sexual relationship with the good-looking young man. Nabarzanes brought this slave as a gift to Alexander, and Bagoas pled, successfully, that Alexander show mercy to Nabarzanes. Curtius goes on to say that Bagoas remained with Alexander and eventually provided sexual services to this new king, too.

§4.

Ancient concepts of sexuality and sexual practices are subjects that scholars have debated intensely in recent times. How to understand Alexander's sexuality has been even more interesting and even more controversial to scholars. The only point of agreement in these debates is that ancient attitudes were very different from modern ones, and that the terms we use to understand and discuss sexuality do not work well when we try to understand and discuss sex in the ancient world. For example, the modern term "homosexuality" and its relatives seem most often to refer to states of being: one is either "homosexual," "heterosexual," or perhaps "bisexual." These terms seem anachronistic if used to describe ancient Macedonians and Greeks. For example, an Athenian man during the Classical period might have a publicly known and accepted sexual relationship with a younger man, but also an ongoing sexual relationship, marriage, and family life with his wife. "Bisexual" does not describe this state of affairs well, because this mature Athenian man would avoid an acknowledged sexual relationship with another man of his own age and free status, but he might not think twice about demanding sex from a household slave of either sex. No slave could refuse sexual advances from her or his master, so for a slave the notion of "sexuality" seems to be practically meaningless. Women's sexuality was also complex and diverse. A free Athenian woman's sexual choices were very strictly limited to the sphere of marriage, so for her, a general concept of "individuated sexuality" seems to make little sense. Adult women in Sparta, by contrast, could openly and agreeably have children by men not their husband and affairs with adolescent girls. Of course, in the Persian royal court no subordinate had any power to refuse the Great King, whatever he wanted to do.

To complicate the situation even further, the sources reveal that only *some* Greek communities agreed that sexual relations between free male citizens were socially and legally acceptable between an older "lover" and a younger "beloved" (to translate the Greek terms). And everywhere Greeks emphatically believed that the relationship was acceptable and honorable *only* if the mature lover used the relationship to help educate the adolescent beloved in the ways of the world, in how to become a respected and effective citizen in his city-state. The relationship would not last beyond the time when the beloved became mature and ready to operate on his own socially and politically. So, the relationship was defined as much in terms of age, social position, and political status as by gender or biological sex. While some communities celebrated such relationships, others merely tolerated them, and others condemned them outright. According to the laws and definitions of many modern nations, such relationships would certainly count as sexual child abuse. It is even plausible that the Macedonian elite sometimes engaged in brother-sister marriage, as certainly happened in Egypt, and today that custom would count as incest. In short, modern comparisons offer little help in interpreting how sex, in all its complexities, contributed to, detracted from, or shaped the lives of ancient Macedonians and Greeks.

It is a modern preoccupation with sexual identity that drives scholars and others to discuss whether Alexander was, in modern terms, heterosexual, homosexual, or bisexual. Neither Alexander nor anyone he encountered in his life would have thought to ask that question in those terms. The modern discussion is also fueled in part by the fact that Alexander did not marry until relatively late in his life, as if the decision to marry was somehow an indication of sexual passion in his world. In fact, marriages served mainly to cement relationships between families and produce heirs to inherit family property and power. Arranged marriages, then as now, could – and often did – develop into love matches between spouses, but that is not why marriage existed in the ancient world. In any case, the ancient sources were certain that Alexander was sexually active with women. When Barsine, the daughter of a prominent Persian and a Greek woman, and the widow of Memnon of

Rhodes, was captured in 333 and brought to Alexander, he was reportedly so entranced by her beauty – and her high-level knowledge of Greek literature – that he became her lover. Plutarch asserted that Barsine was the only woman with whom Alexander had sex before his (first) marriage several years later, but other sources report that he had learned about sex from Pancaste, a woman from Thessaly in Greece so beautiful that Apelles the painter became famous for his nude portrait of her. Our sources also recount that Alexander, like the Persian kings he replaced, regularly took his pick of the many concubines kept at court as temporary sex partners. Most colorfully of all, they also report that Alexander spent thirteen days having sex with the female leader of a tribe of women warriors ("Amazons"), who came to him from the Caucasus region, asking that he impregnate her so she could have his child.

The ancient sources do not report, however, what modern scholars have asserted: that Alexander and his very close friend Hephaestion were lovers. Achilles and his equally close friend Patroclus provided the legendary model for this friendship, but Homer in the *Iliad* never suggested that they had sex with each other. (That came from later authors.) If Alexander and Hephaestion did have a sexual relationship, it would have been transgressive by majority Greek standards because they were the same age, not an older "lover" and a significantly younger "beloved." Whatever description we give of Alexander's sexuality, and no modern label seems to fit, the most significant point is that seeking sexual pleasure was not an obsession, or even a driving force, in his life. It seems clear that, as Plutarch insists, Alexander was, by the measure of his culture, restrained in his sexual urges and behaviors and not dominated by a need to pursue sexual pleasure. This also fits with everything else we see about Alexander's character from his actions in other aspects of his life: when aimed at a goal, no concerns of pleasure, comfort, or safety meant anything to him; at moments of leisure, on the other hand, he could give himself over for a time to indulgences (in sex, in wine, in anger). This made him like Dionysus.

§5.

Alexander paused in his pursuit of the treacherous and murderous Bessus to pass judgment on two groups that were brought before him. The first were the Greek mercenaries who had accepted employment with the Persian king. The second were ambassadors from Greek states who had been captured on their way to pay their respects to, and negotiate with, Darius while he was still on the throne of his empire. Alexander's decisions once again show the extreme value he placed on loyalty. Those Greeks who had joined the Persian army before Philip formalized his Greek alliance Alexander let go free; those who had joined afterward Alexander compelled to continue to serve in his own army. Those ambassadors who came from Greek communities formerly under Persian rule he released; those from Athens and Sparta he kept under guard. These last men, whom their home cities had dispatched to negotiate with the Persian king, were disturbing evidence of a rebellion in Greece that could break out anew at any time. But Alexander never hesitated in his drive forward and eastward, never considering for a moment a return home to ensure stability. His goal lay in the other direction.

If his army had any doubt about the king's commitment, he destroyed it on the eve of departure. He commanded his men to collect all the transport wagons carrying the heaps and heaps of plunder from their many victories, small and large. Alexander took a burning torch, approached his own pile of prizes, and set it ablaze. He then ordered all the rest to burn, too. The men stood stunned, before the example of the king's personal sacrifice moved them to follow suit. Encumbered with only the base essentials for a fast campaign over hard country, they proclaimed themselves ready to set off with discipline and enthusiasm on an expedition into hostile, unknown lands that promised challenges more difficult than anything they had encountered thus far. As for Alexander, Plutarch reports that he included among his own essential equipment copies of the great works of Greek literature. While preparing the army's draft animals, food stores, and weapons, he also commissioned new copies of the works of poets and dramatists, including the plays of Euripides, to take with him on his journey deeper into Asia.

§6.

As he set out, in the second half of 330, the first of the journey's challenges presented itself, but behind him, not in front. While on the first stage of his march, he received word that the former Persian satrap Satibarzanes had rebelled against the new Macedonian regime. In keeping with his policies of empire, Alexander had reinstated Satibarzanes in his position in the region called Aria, establishing a small military garrison to keep the peace and ensure loyalty. But now the satrap had betrayed Alexander's trust and massacred the garrison's commander and his soldiers. It is possible that the king's public demonstration of an unwavering commitment to progress eastward had given the Persian a false impression; Alexander's plans lay forward, but this was treachery and betrayal. He picked a mobile rapid-response force and marched to Aria so quickly that Satibarzanes could not hope to resist but fled in a panic to Bessus in Bactria. Despite his eagerness to be on his way, Alexander spent a month re-establishing the satrapy, ruthlessly punishing everyone who had conspired with the disloyal governor. Significantly, however, even after this rebellion Alexander stuck to his policy: he appointed another Persian to take Satibarzanes' place. Alexander's commitment to the new world he was creating was unshakeable.

Sensing potential cracks in the security of his new order that were too serious to overlook, he did more to shore up his new empire. He turned southeastward to make sure of his control of the regions of Drangiana and Arachosia (today on the borders of Iran, Pakistan, and Afghanistan). In Drangiana, he faced the most shocking challenge yet: a plot against his own life, not by unhappy Persians, but among the Macedonians closest to him. No Macedonian was ever surprised when a royal heir's rivals undertook violence to unseat him during the period of succession; Alexander had faced this threat when Philip died and had acted with swift, confident, murderous assurance to forestall all dangers to himself as the new king. But in a campaigning army, thousands of miles from home, amid a string of victories, a plot against a well-established king was unprecedented. To Alexander, who placed loyalty at the pinnacle of all virtues, it was unthinkable.

The course of this episode in Alexander's life was messy and complicated. At its heart was Philotas, a prominent young commander who was also the son of Parmenion, the experienced general whom Alexander had stationed back west in Media to manage the empire while the king and his army moved east. A lovers' spat between two men in the Macedonian army resulted in one of them informing Philotas that there was a plot to kill Alexander. Philotas failed to pass the message on to Alexander, never telling his informant why he remained silent. The informant was frantic, fearing that any delay might cause the death of the king, and he found a way to pass the message to Alexander directly. Alexander reacted at once: he sent armed guards to arrest the man identified as the assassin, who was killed when he drew a sword to resist arrest. His death made it impossible to verify the extent of the conspiracy. The crisis grew. Alexander arrested Philotas, on the grounds that he had failed to warn his king of the danger. Philotas stood trial before the army; his defense was that he judged the news of a plot to be merely an empty rumor, concocted by a scorned lover seeking revenge for rejection. Philotas' reputation harmed his cause, since he was widely known and disliked for being arrogant and for showing off the tremendous wealth he had acquired during his campaigns. Philotas' personal enemies had for some time spread word that Philotas made critical and even disloyal remarks about Alexander. The trial was marked by anger on all sides, and perhaps by Alexander's memory of Philotas' role in the Pixodarus fiasco back home. Philotas finally confessed under torture and suffered the traditional fate of a traitor: his fellow soldiers stoned him to death.

Others in Alexander's inner circle also stood trial and were acquitted for lack of evidence. From our distance, it is impossible to know if these acquittals indicated the fair workings of justice, or political manipulation aimed at keeping as many influential Macedonians as possible on the king's side. In any case, the affair did not lead to an indiscriminate massacre of anyone with a possible claim to royal power, and in this it was a departure from Macedonian tradition.

§7.

What happened next was definitely political. First, Alexander the king ordered the trial of Alexander of Lyncestis, who had been under guard for three years under suspicion of aiming to seize power after Philip's death. The Lyncestian was dragged before the army to be tried at last. His fear prevented him from speaking effectively, and he was condemned to die. Alexander of Lyncestis had not been much of a threat to Alexander's position; his main crime was that his bloodline made him eligible to rule as king. The greater threat was Parmenion, the father of Philotas who had died under the stones of Alexander's army. By Macedonian custom, Parmenion could be expected to seek revenge, regardless of his son's guilt or innocence. Therefore it was particularly worrisome that Parmenion was stationed in a position of considerable power and independence to Alexander's rear in Media. He had access to soldiers and to the Persian treasuries. He was a member of the Macedonian social elite with reputation as a soldier, general, and astute political actor. Most importantly, Parmenion commanded the respect of the army. He would be a serious threat to Alexander if he proved disloyal, and in the aftermath of this plot against the king's life, his loyalty was certainly in question.

Alexander could not overlook the danger of a man who could seize power, hold it, leave him and his expeditionary force cut off in the wilds of eastern Persia, and style himself king of the Macedonians. At the very least, putting down such a rebellion would take months and delay Alexander's eastward ambitions indefinitely. So Alexander acted with decision, in keeping with his character, and with violence, in keeping with the traditions of Macedonian royal politics. He sent one of his Companions – disguised in Arab clothing and riding on a camel – on a rushed journey to Ecbatana carrying letters that authorized the death of Parmenion without trial. This messenger covered 800 miles of desert at a feverish pace; he arrived before the eleventh day, and more importantly, before any news of the trial and execution of Philotas. As Parmenion read the letter, Alexander's man finished his mission, striking off the head of the man who had served as a respected comrade-in-arms and advisor to Alexander and his father before him. The old general's death was a murder that Alexander cannot have ordered casually. The man was a distinguished military leader whose death would certainly anger many in the army. Alexander and Parmenion had disagreed on military decisions in the past, even clashed at times, but nothing in the old man's record justified his summary execution, at least not by some modern notions of justice. The justification in Alexander's world came from the violent reality of power politics among the Macedonian elite and Alexander's willingness to act in accordance with those norms whenever he suspected any possible disloyalty, any threat at all to his superiority. In that choice, he was a man of his time and place driven by his internal vision of being literally unique in the world.

§8.

By now Alexander was right to think that many of his fellow Macedonians – both among the general ranks of troops and among the inner circle closest to the king – were bitterly angry with him. The heart of the problem was his new and expanding policy as King of Asia (no longer merely King of the Macedonians), according to which he placed his former Persian enemies into administrative offices. Macedonians had fought, bled, and died to conquer territories that Persians were now ruling. What brought this anger to a boiling point was the power of symbols, which draw people's attention to specifics while affecting their perceptions and attitudes most broadly. The symbols that especially infuriated the Macedonians and Greeks around Alexander were the king's own clothes, and the protocols that now determined everyone's behavior in the royal court. Alexander tried to blend the ways of his own heritage with a strong dose of Persian customs. Instead of the plain tunic usually worn by Macedonian men, Alexander began to wear a white robe and belt in the Persian style. He also took to wearing around his head a purple band of fabric interwoven with white threads, the so-called "diadem" of Persian royalty. He required his Companions to wear Persian-styled cloaks with purple borders, and he outfitted their horses in livery that had a Persian look. It is easy to see why. In order to rule Asia as King of Asia, Alexander needed to appear to the people of Asia as they expected a king to appear. The people constantly surrounding the king were part of his "costume" and had to look the part as well. It is also easy to see why the Macedonians and Greeks would object: they were the victors, but were being asked to look (somewhat) like the vanquished.

Realizing that these symbolic concessions to cultural blending were controversial, to say the least, Alexander carefully avoided crossing certain lines. He did not wear long sleeves, in the Persian custom. And he did not adopt the most distinctive (to Europeans) and offensive (to Greeks and Macedonians) piece of barbarian clothing: pants. As Plutarch observes, Alexander mixed his clothing in a novel combination, to show that he was not privileging one style over the other but creating a new style to symbolize the new world he was working to invent.

Alexander also devised a new set of protocols for his court, new at least for a king of the Macedonians. Persians were given jobs as royal attendants, and Darius' brother was given special prominence as one of his bodyguards, a position in the past reserved for the Macedonian elite. Alexander even put together a harem of concubines chosen from the most beautiful women in Asia, from whom he reportedly chose a different partner to sleep with each night throughout the year, just as the Persian kings before him had customarily done. In his new protocols, as with his new way of dressing, Alexander aimed to avoid imposing on his Greeks and Macedonians the custom of the Persian court that was most offensive to them. This was the tradition of people lying facedown on the ground – "falling down" (*proskynesis*), as the Greeks called it – when they entered into the presence of the king, as a physical sign of their respect for his superior status. This prostration Alexander asked only of Persians and other Asians accustomed to this tradition. He did not object if Greeks or Macedonians decided to prostrate themselves, but he did not require it of them.

No matter how carefully Alexander tried to achieve moderation between his traditions and the new ways, his "mixed" customs did not sit well with many Macedonians and Greeks. Instead of seeing the mixing as symbolizing something new and valid on its own terms, as a fundamental aspect of the way Alexander was choosing to rule as King of Asia (and more), they interpreted his changes as blatant maneuvers aimed at the eventual obliteration of their treasured traditions. They feared that the new, combined traditions pointed the way, sooner rather than later, to the imposition of purely barbarian and Asiatic ways of life and rule. What Alexander saw as a creative compromise, they saw as a slippery slope. In addition, they worried that the changes could only mean further expansion of their king's policy of relying on former enemies as his governors and supporters. As Alexander moved further east, they knew, he was going into territory and among diverse peoples of which Greeks and Macedonians had almost no certain knowledge. They had at least known something about Persia and the peoples in the Persian Empire from the long and much written-about history of interaction between Greeks, Macedonians, and Persians, and therefore they could claim to be able to use that knowledge to help them serve as effective administrators of former Persian imperial possessions. But in the lands where Alexander was planning to go now, they would be completely at sea, so to speak, ignorant of local ways that first-rate administrators needed to know to govern safely and productively. It stood to reason for them to fear that in these new places Alexander would want to rely even more, or even exclusively, on people from those regions who offered their loyalty to him. For these reasons, many Macedonians and Greeks were apprehensive about their place in the new world, and their fears were worsened, not lessened, by each symbolic innovation that Alexander added to their way of life in these ever more strange (to them) lands. Their anxiety had nowhere to go except climb higher as the expedition proceeded; they knew full well that Alexander was not going to turn back the clock.

§9.

Aware of this undercurrent of anger and apprehension, Alexander distributed lavish gifts to as many people as possible to try to ease their discontent. He then threw himself back to the task of constructing the future. His energy was so high, in fact, that over the winter of 330–329 he discarded the usual, cautious practice of ancient commanders, who invariably put their armies into camps for the winter, to minimize attrition from bad weather, cold temperatures, and scarce food. Alexander built a town and named it "Getting Out in Front" (*Prophthasia*). The name commemorated his success in getting ahead of the conspirators who sought to assassinate him. Moving up the long valley of the Helmand River in the Hindu Kush mountains, bordering on Afghanistan, he encountered the Ariaspians, a people honored by the Persian kings for having supported Cyrus, the founder of the Persian Empire. Alexander declared that the Ariaspians could remain free because they had, two centuries before, remained loyal to their sovereign. Arriving in Arachosia, he appointed a non-Persian to the governorship, perhaps to show his doubters that his new policy of rule was meant to include and reward everyone, regardless of their origins. Marching north, he founded another new settlement in Afghanistan, named Alexandria; this city came to be known by the Arabic version of that name, "Iskandariya", and eventually by its current name, "Kandahar."

§10.

From Kandahar, Alexander showed the unbeatable resolve that drove him forward. In the middle of a savage Afghan winter, he drove his army over the mountain passes into the territory of the Paropamisadans. The snow fell so heavily that it blinded the troops, and they suffered the agonies of frostbite on their hands and on the feet that carried them along this wild path. Mittens and boots were never standard issue for armies trained to fight under the Mediterranean sun. Unable to find food in the drifts, the men had to eat raw fish they splashed out of the icy rivers, to gnaw on weeds, and, finally, to butcher their mules for meat. The stress of pain, fatigue, and hunger made the soldiers susceptible to fatal hypothermia. As the army was on the verge of collapse, they spotted plumes of smoke spiraling up from what looked to be banks of snow. These proved to be the chimney-holes of buried houses, the dwellings of the local people gifted with generations of experience surviving winters like this. These people gave Alexander's army sufficient supplies to keep them alive and moving until Alexander, with constant encouragement, could guide them down and out of the snow.

Nothing could make him stop pushing on, not even the news that Satibarzanes had returned to Aria with 2,000 Bactrian cavalry to raise a rebellion. Alexander broke off a unit to turn back and deal with the rebel. When this force met Satibarzanes on the battlefield, Satibarzanes snatched off his helmet and dared the Macedonians to send a champion to fight him one on one. Erygius, one of Alexander's Companions whose white hair showed his age, took up the challenge. Erygius got the better of the fight and stabbed Satibarzanes through the neck with his spear. The barbarian did not fall, but fought on. Erygius, fighting now with his sword, thrust it past the Persian's guard and into his face. Satibarzanes, in agony but still evidently fearless, clutched the sword and pushed it deeper, ending his own life and the rebellion. Erygius returned to Alexander with the Persian's head as a trophy. Alexander himself led his army forward in search of Bessus, who waited with 7,000 men amid "scorched earth" to block Alexander's way into Bactria. The Macedonian army once again "got out in front" with a forced march that probably took them through the snow-filled wasteland of the Khawak Pass. His army, in sandals and tunics, eating only the food they carried, ascended the rocky and barren mountains through deep drifts to the narrow pass at 12,000 feet, gasping from the lack of oxygen at that altitude.

They made the fifty-mile trek in fifteen days, a superhuman effort given the extreme conditions. Just as Alexander's unexpected appearance had panicked the Thebans in 335, his arrival in Bactria in 329 startled Bessus so badly that he retreated northward across the Oxus (Amu Darya) River into the satrapy of Sogdiana (today Uzbekistan). Alexander gained control of Bactria with force and diplomacy, appointed a new satrap to govern the region for him, and set out in pursuit of Bessus. The fugitive pretender expected that the river Oxus would buy him time, since Alexander had no boats to ferry his army across. But this campaign was shaping up to be a review of Alexander's tactical history, and once again he set his army to making pontoons out of hides stuffed with hay, crossed the river, and continued his pursuit.

§11.

On the northern side of the Oxus, Alexander stumbled upon a town whose inhabitants welcomed him and claimed that they were Greeks! They said they were members of the Branchidai, a priestly clan that Xerxes as Persian King had moved from Miletus on the coast of Anatolia to this location on the eastern frontier of his empire long ago in 479. According to Curtius, the move had been necessary because the townspeople's ancestors had helped Xerxes sack the sanctuary and oracle at Didyma that it was their ancestral duty to protect, and the king was taking them as far away as possible from Miletus to prevent their being destroyed by its outraged citizens.

Alexander had troops from Miletus in his army, and he asked them what should happen to these descendants of ancient traitors and religious criminals. The Milesians could not agree on a suitable response. Alexander then made the decision: the inhabitants were killed, and every trace of their town was obliterated, from the foundation of their walls to the roots of their trees. The time and effort, the ferocity that it took to eradicate this place from the face of the earth, show with unmistakable clarity how deeply Alexander valued loyalty and piety. To defend those qualities and to exact revenge for betrayal of them, no punishment was too brutal. The weight of justice was crushing and fatal, and no one expected it to be any other way.

Over the course of Alexander's wars, in Europe and Asia, his speed and aggression always served him well, both on the battlefield and by sowing chaos and dismay among his enemies. Once again, his swift arrival destroyed any confidence that Bessus' allies might have had, and that erosion of confidence bred treachery. The Sogdian tribal leader Spitamenes sent Alexander a message saying that he would hand over Bessus. Alexander dispatched his Companion Ptolemy to pick up the prisoner. Spitamenes feared that his treachery would be rewarded with treachery – with justification; everyone was learning about Alexander's attitudes toward loyalty – so he left Bessus naked and bound in a wooden collar, and fled before Ptolemy arrived. Ptolemy dragged the prisoner back to Alexander's camp.

7

MURDER, MARRIAGE, AND MIXING CUSTOMS IN AFGHANISTAN (329 TO 327 BC)

§1.

The satrapy of Bactria (Afghanistan) occupied the northeastern corner of the Persian Empire, as distant from Persepolis as Persepolis was from Macedonia. The Bactrian peoples were toughened by their environment, which was blazing hot on its upland plains, freezing cold in its mountain heights, and largely dry as a bone, except for occasional rivers that gouged channels through rock and sand. In this land, conquest would be hard, and rule would be harder.

To bring Bactria into his empire, Alexander made a remarkable decision in late 329, upon reaching the city of Bactra (today Balkh), the capital of the satrapy and according to legend the most ancient city in the world. Bactra was famous as sacred to the religion of the Persian kings, which is today called Zoroastrianism after its founding prophet, Zoroaster. Zoroastrian believers worshipped Ahura Mazda as the supreme deity of the universe. He was the source of all good, and his worshippers prayed constantly for his victory, for this god was in perpetual battle against evil. Fire was sacred in the Zoroastrian faith, and its priests nurtured flames kept burning and pure in the temples. To pollute a fire was sacrilege, and there was nothing more polluted than a corpse. Accordingly, the people of Bactria did not burn their dead, as the Macedonians and Greeks often did, according to their own notions of respect for the deceased. Instead, the inhabitants of Bactra kept dogs whose role was to eat the dying and the dead, whose bodies were left lying in the streets of the city. They called these animals "Undertakers."

When Alexander and his men entered this legendary city, they had to march past, over, and around growling dogs chewing on mangled, bloody, stinking, and rotting human beings. This sight was profoundly disturbing, especially to Alexander, who knew well the opening lines of the *Iliad*, where the poet sings of the fate every hero feared as much as the disgrace of being branded a coward while alive: being dishonored by having his dead body cast out to be "food for dogs, and meals for birds." The scene in the streets of Bactra was more shocking to him yet, for the undertaker dogs feasted not only on corpses already dead, but on the still-living bodies of the elderly and chronically ill, banished by their younger or healthier families to the streets to end their days torn by animals. Alexander ordered the "Undertakers" destroyed, decreeing an end to this local funerary custom (though later archaeological evidence suggests that the custom at some point came back into use).

Never yet on his journey of conquest had Alexander attempted to impose changes in the way of life or religious beliefs and practices of the many peoples whose lands he had conquered. He did not order mandatory worship of Greek gods or demolition of local temples; he did not decree Greek to be the "official" language of his empire or order changes in local dress. He recognized that to impose different cultural norms would cause social unrest and needless resentment, undermining his plans to rule an empire vaster and more diverse than even had the Persian kings. He knew from reading Herodotus that Cyrus the Great, the founder of the Persian Empire, had profited from the popular support that he gained by allowing conquered peoples to follow their own customs and religion; by contrast, Cyrus' successor Cambyses, who outraged local sacred traditions, had harmed his ability to rule effectively. Moreover, Alexander's having appointed Persians to governing positions in his new empire demonstrated that he would not follow

Aristotle's instruction that Greeks should rule barbarians as slaves and treat them like animals. And even if his Persian officials could be seen as exceptions because they were members of their society's elite and had enjoyed the benefit of sophisticated educations, Alexander had previously made clear his rejection of his teacher's view.

§2.

The year before, when the news reached his army that Bessus had murdered Darius, the rumor spread like wildfire among the ranks that the war was over and Alexander was preparing to take them back to Macedonia. The soldiers joyfully began packing up to go home. Alexander was of course already determined to proceed to India, so he assembled the troops to persuade them to keep going. Curtius, who loves to season his narrative with dramatic speeches (composed in his own words, of course) devotes more than a few paragraphs to Alexander's arguments urging his men to stick with him. Alexander succeeds. He explains to the soldiers that the barbarians were very different from Macedonians and Greeks in their religion, culture, and language, and that their lack of "civilization" reflects their always having lived like wild animals confined by authoritarian masters. It would take time, he explains, for them to be "tamed." Freedom, in contact with Macedonians and Greeks, would educate them to live as free men should. The vocabulary of Alexander's speech perhaps reflected his need to convince men who saw barbarians as inferior (which was Curtius' view), but Alexander's main point was clear: barbarians could, given the opportunity, become the cultural peers of Macedonians and Greeks in his new empire.

In this speech, Alexander did not specify whether this process of "civilizing" barbarians should take place through a natural evolution, as it were, with the barbarians learning by observing how Macedonians and Greeks lived, or if it should be aggressively promoted, by his requiring changes in the barbarians' customs. It is clear that Alexander was willing to impose carefully considered cultural changes on his own followers when he thought the time was right, as he did when he required his companions to adopt the mixed Macedonian/Greek/Persian mode of clothing that he pioneered. The key point is that Alexander's change in his clothing was a "mixture," not an obliteration of one way of life to be completely replaced by an alien one. The same was true of his prohibition on "Undertakers" in Bactra. He forbade that particular custom, but he left the rest of the city's religious and social traditions undisturbed. In that way, his decision created another "mixture" of customs, not the complete suppression of long-established local beliefs and practices by the forceful imposition of a totally Macedonian and Greek way of life.

§3.

With the weather in the late autumn worsening, Alexander led his army from Bactra north into Sogdiana, advancing to the Jaxartes River (Syr Darya). Here he captured the border forts that the Persians had built to defend the river crossings against the nomadic Massagetae on the opposite banks. One of these was Cyropolis, named after Cyrus, the first Persian king. Since Cyropolis resisted Alexander's assault, he made an example by killing every one of its male defenders and enslaving its women and children. This was not the only lesson he aimed to teach. The Massagetae were a warrior tribe of Scythians, well known to all educated Greeks from the accounts in Herodotus. The historian told the story of how Tomyris, the queen of the Massagetae, had not only outwitted and slaughtered Cyrus' invading army, killing the king in the process, but had decapitated Cyrus and dunked his head in a wineskin filled with human blood, a supreme act of contempt. Alexander would push his army into Sogdiana, "going beyond" his Persian predecessor, marching deeper into Scythia than even the great Cyrus, seeking a victory where the greatest of the Great Kings had met defeat, death, and humiliation.

The Massagetae were difficult opponents, skilled in fighting from horseback, without permanent cities to attack. Facing this formidable challenge, Alexander learned of another. News came that Spitamenes had laid siege to Maracanda (Samarkand), in the Macedonian army's rear. Alexander was intent on crossing the Jaxartes, so he split off a small force to quell what he thought was a limited threat behind him. He may even have thought that the siege could be lifted through negotiation instead of battle, as he sent an interpreter along in a leading role to make contact with the enemy.

The Scythian tribesmen had gathered on the opposite bank of the river, hurling insults across. Alexander built a fortified settlement called "Alexandria the Furthest" (*Alexandria Eschatē*) for defensive and symbolic purposes – no Persian had ever done as much – and used his "stuffed-hide ferrying" technique to get his men across the river. He led the attack himself, breaking out his field artillery to rain missiles down on the men in the enemy's battle line; usually such weapons were employed only to batter fortifications. These innovative tactics drove the enemy from the riverbanks. The Massagetae opposed his landing by riding around and around Alexander's men, loosing volleys of arrows as the Macedonians scrambled off their makeshift boats and onto the shore. Alexander deployed his archers, slingers, and cavalry to force back the enemy, forming a beachhead with combined arms that routed the Scythians and saw his army safely ashore. Despite the Scythians' vaunted mobility, more than a thousand perished before they could ride away.

§4.

In his drive to follow up his victory and "go beyond," Alexander pushed his army hard in pursuit of the fleeing Scythians. They marched on through arid country made even harsher by soaring temperatures. The men were parched, and desperate for water they drank from brackish sources that they would have ordinarily passed by. Diarrhea began raging through the army, and Alexander himself became so ill that he nearly died. He had to be carried back to camp, putting an end to the pursuit. A Scythian chief then sent a messenger saying it had been wrong of him to attack and asking for a truce; Alexander was too sick to refuse the offer. Arrian, showing insight into Alexander's characteristic motivation, remarks that Alexander would have considered it disgraceful not to resume the punitive expedition against the Scythians if he had judged them to be untrustworthy.

As Alexander was recovering, awful news arrived: Spitamenes had destroyed the men he had sent to relieve the siege of Maracanda. Alexander's appointed commander had failed to maintain battlefield discipline, and the resulting slaughter was both a devastating loss of manpower and a blot on Alexander's record as commander-in-chief. He swiftly assembled an elite force, which he marched 180 miles in three days and a night, but Spitamenes escaped before he arrived. The winter was now too harsh to fight on, so Alexander had to return to Bactra. There, he reorganized his forces to give them even more flexibility, the better to match the highly mobile tactics of his new adversaries. The Scythians lived off the land, moving freely around their country with their herds of cattle, adeptly avoiding battle except under conditions of their choosing. War with them was like chasing ghosts, even for a tactician of Alexander's skill and imagination.

§5.

While Alexander waited out the snow and cold, ambassadors arrived from the northern barbarians. First came Scythians, who offered Alexander a princess to marry. Then came others who proposed a joint military campaign deeper into the steppes. Alexander thanked both, but declined the offers. He was bound for India, he told them, to expand his conquest of Asia. He said that he would return, but only by way of Greece once he had attained the far eastern reaches of the continent. It is difficult to picture the ideas of geography that informed Alexander's vision, and the ancient sources do not explain them. Alexander's geography probably derived from that of Aristotle. He (and others) taught that the earth was a sphere, and perhaps Alexander believed that he could cross Asia from west to east and then return to Europe by traveling on in the same direction.

Or, he may have believed that the European-Asian continent was surrounded by a band of sea, Ocean as Greeks named it, and that he could thus sail this endless river back to Europe around a spherical earth. Whatever Alexander thought about the configuration of the continents, his decision not to proceed northward (or southward) also corresponded to a notion explained by Aristotle: the civilized section of the earth was a horizontal band extending west to east around the globe. The regions to the north and south of that sector were too cold or too hot for anything except the roughest-living barbarians. For Alexander, there was only one path to forge. Dionysus and Heracles, the god-men of Greek mythology, had linked Europe and Asia through journeys of conquest, and Alexander could only "go beyond" them by crossing India.

Before he continued, Alexander had one last duty to perform as the successor to the last Persian Great King, Darius. In early 328 he ordered Bessus to be dragged before a public gathering. There Alexander punished him as a traitor according to the Persian royal tradition: the usurper's nose and the tips of his ears were sliced off. This agonizing disfigurement served as a visible and permanent humiliation, a sign that the criminal was unworthy to be a Persian king, who tradition demanded be a handsome, unblemished man. Bessus was sent back to Persia in chains, there to face execution as the disgraced murderer of a king. Arrian criticized the bloody mutilation of Bessus as a "barbarian" act, unworthy of Alexander, and accused the Macedonian king of failing to win a "victory over himself." Alexander, however, knew from reading Herodotus that this was the appropriate punishment according to Persian standards, and that it would be expected of a king to inflict it. Darius I had in fact inscribed on a mountain side for all to see at Bisitun (near Kermanshah in Iran) what he did to traitors: "I cut off his nose, ears, and tongue, and I put out one of his eyes … Then I had him spitted on a post." Alexander regarded Bessus' fate as perfectly fitting not only by Persian tradition, but also through his hatred of a subordinate's disloyalty, the worst crime Alexander could imagine.

§6.

In Herodotus' account of eastern lands Alexander had read that the people of India numbered the largest population in the world. He spent the whole summer of 328 in military actions aimed at increasing security in Sogdiana and Bactria to provide security in his wake. Some of these he led personally, some he delegated. Spitamenes proved an elusive foe and had strengthened his position through alliances with Bactrians and tribes of the Massagetae. Only late in that year or early in the next could Alexander's men force Spitamenes into a pitched battle and smash his cavalry. Spitamenes fled to the steppes, but his former Massagetae allies, hoping to please Alexander and win his pardon, betrayed him, cut off his head, and sent it to Alexander. Alexander captured Spitamenes' family, too, but treated them kindly, as he had treated the family of Darius. Perhaps Alexander respected Spitamenes' dedication, his determination to fight to keep his region free from invaders. Alexander had truly taken to heart Aristotle's lessons about the nobility of courage.

Alcoholic Drinks

People of all ages in the Mediterranean region drank fermented alcoholic beverages as a staple food at nearly every meal. The (mildly) antiseptic effect of the alcohol made the drinks safer from bacterial contamination than water, and the calories were welcome in a world in which many people could afford only a sparse diet. Wine was thought to help in treating illnesses such as fever.

Wine was made from grapes throughout Greece, and from dates in eastern Mediterranean lands. Beer was common in Egypt, and mead (fermented honey) in northern Europe. Greeks often flavored their wine with spices or honey and usually diluted it heavily with water. They thought that drinking undiluted wine was dangerous because it could induce mad-ness. Even heavily diluted wine could make men drunk when they kept downing cups for hours at the *symposia* (drink-ing parties) that were a favorite evening activity. A favorite drinking game was to use drinking cups, which were usually shallow bowls with handles, to fling the dregs of the wine gathered at the bottom of the cup at a target – or at other drinkers.

Aristotle identified two different levels of drunkenness in his analysis of drinking's effect on different personalities: (1) "drunk," meaning "nearly passed out and unable to decide or act," and (2) "with one's torso topped off," meaning "too drunk to make good decisions but not aware of being seriously impaired." The second condition was dangerous because these drinkers were prone to take rash actions they later regretted. Alexander's life offered tragic examples of the truth of Aristotle's insight.

In the fall of 328, another incident revealed that Alexander remained lethally liable to the danger that Aristotle warned about: the toxic combination of alcohol and anger. Alexander had appointed Cleitus as satrap of Bactria and Sogdiana; this was a key element in his strategy to ensure that his conquests were secure behind him as he advanced eastward. He chose Cleitus as a respected commander with personal ties to him. Cleitus had decades of experience in the field, having begun his career under Philip II. His sister had been Alexander's nurse when he was an infant, and Alexander was said to love her like a mother. Finally, Alexander owed Cleitus his life: at the Battle of the Granicus River, it was Cleitus who slashed off the arm of the Persian who was about to bring his sword down on Alexander's head. Greece's most famous painter, Apelles, had commemorated this moment of Cleitus' heroism by painting a portrait of him on horseback.

Cleitus, however, had been nursing a grudge, which surfaced on a fateful night in Maracanda. The occasion was a party in

the standard Macedonian tradition, an evening of hard drinking. Alexander hosted the celebration, which he declared to be
in honor of Castor and Pollux, the mythological twins whose
heroic deeds earned them immortality among the stars. Our
sources disagree about what happened, and any reconstruction
is open to question. The party continued deep into the night,
with everyone drinking heavily and continuously. Some of the
partiers began to proclaim in drunken voices that Alexander's
deeds were already greater than those of the divine heroes, whose
honor the party had been pledging with bowl after bowl of wine.
Arrian says that they also mentioned Heracles, insisting that the
jealousy of lesser men denied this hero his due honor while he
was still alive. Plutarch adds that a poet, hired to accompany
the army, began reciting a comic poem of his own composi-
tion, poking fun at the Macedonian sub-commanders who had
been bested on the battlefield by barbarians. Some of the guests,
offended, started to object loudly, but Alexander ordered the
poet to continue his recitation. At some point, someone (Curtius says it was Alexander) blurted out that Philip had accomplished nothing compared to his son. All this shameless flattery
and adulation of the young king proved too much for Cleitus
to bear. He was as drunk as anyone, and always a hothead,
quick to anger and with biting criticism of others. Now, his self-
control long since drowned by alcohol, Cleitus protested that
comparing Alexander to a god was improper, and anyway it was
disgraceful to mock Macedonians in the presence of barbarians
(he meant the Persians in Alexander's entourage and administra-
tion). Those dead Macedonians were lucky, he snarled, who had
not lived to see this day, when they would have to beg Persians
for permission to speak to their king. And, he continued, as for
the new empire of Alexander, it was a hopeless task to be satrap
of Sogdiana, where the people were nothing but bloodthirsty
wild animals who could never be mastered by force, let alone
governed. He went on to the dangerous subject of the murders of
Attalus and Parmenion, and then raised the ante even further by
mentioning Philip: it was dishonorable to denigrate the former
king – Cleitus had served with him and could testify first-hand

to Philip's valor – and to ignore the Macedonian blood that the troops had shed to win Alexander his list of victories. The glory belonged to the soldiers; they were the ones who made you so great, he sneered in Alexander's face, that you can deny your own father and pretend to be the son of Ammon!

Alexander had only one epithet when he was at the extremity of rage, and he now hurled at Cleitus the supremely contemptuous insult that later Greeks repeated on his example: "You shithead!" ("evil head" in Greek). Cleitus would pay for his insults, Alexander warned, if he kept them up. Cleitus had gone to the brink of what was tolerable from a subordinate, even one as respected and valued as he was. He had shown contempt for Alexander's claims to special status. The job Alexander had entrusted him with– a position of power and responsibility – he condemned as a pointless exercise in futility.

Cleitus' friends tried to drag him away from the party. Their hands were not over his mouth, however, and he shouted out one last crack: Alexander owed his life to him, Cleitus, who rescued him at the Granicus. This, finally, was too much. Cleitus' remark was a claim that Alexander owed him a debt. This particular debt could be repaid, but never surpassed; Alexander could potentially save Cleitus' life, but that would be repayment of equal for equal, and since Cleitus' gift was first, Alexander would inevitably be second. Owing his life to Cleitus compromised the incomparable superiority to others that Alexander believed defined his existence, and now that enduring deficit was being thrown in his face publicly. Leaping up from the couch on which the guests at drinking parties always reclined, Alexander shouted for his guards; realizing their king was drunk and in a rage, they did not respond. Alexander's friends grabbed him and wrestled him back down.

Had the confrontation ended there, with the drunken king and his drunken general restrained by their friends, disaster might have been averted. But Cleitus broke away and burst back into the group. According to Plutarch, he yelled out one line of Greek poetry to Alexander: "Ahhh! Things are being badly run in Greece!" Why would Cleitus tear himself loose to hurl these seemingly vague words at the king? Alexander instantly knew the answer. Cleitus was quoting from the Greek play *Andromache* by Euripides, whose works Alexander loved so much he could act out entire scenes from them from memory. Alexander recognized the allusion: the line was spoken by Peleus, the father of Achilles, in an argument with Menelaus after the fall of Troy. Menelaus was the dishonorable villain, and Peleus in this passage went on to accuse him of being a vain and worthless blowhard stealing glory from the soldiers who had fought, and won, a war for him. These Macedonian soldiers in the wilds of Afghanistan were so steeped in Greek literature that even drunk out of their wits and beside themselves with rage, they could still conduct a complete conversation with a single line of poetry quoted from the Athenian stage.

This line from Euripides pushed Alexander over the edge. He grabbed a spear from one of his guards and smashed it into Cleitus' chest as he tried to stumble away. The drunken victim died on the spot. All sources agree that Alexander immediately regretted the deed. As humiliating as Cleitus' retorts had been, it was also humiliating to find himself a drunken murderer. He pulled the shaft from the dead man's body and tried to stab himself in the neck. His friends stopped him before he could draw blood. Arrian reports that Alexander's remorse at his deed was so profound that he lay in his bed without eating or drinking anything for three days, locked away from everyone in his bottomless grief. Finally, worried that the king would die, his friends broke in on him, begging him to return to them. Arrian says the priests in Alexander's entourage then told him to sacrifice to Dionysus, the god of wine and violence, who had been angry because the party took place on a day sacred to him and should therefore have been in his honor. Plutarch agrees with Arrian that the scholars that Alexander had brought along were also called in to talk to the distraught king. The historian Callisthenes tried to console him with a comforting gentleness, but the philosopher Anaxarchus stormed in with a radically different argument: a true and genuine king, by the very nature of his unquestioned superiority, was the one who determined how things should be run. Whatever he did was by definition the right thing to do.

§7.

The idea forming the focus of Anaxarchus' attempt at persuasion was the very core of the line from Euripides that Cleitus had flung and that had precipitated his death. That idea was *nomos*, a Greek word for a complex cluster of meanings. In some contexts, *nomos* means "custom" or "what is conventionally agreed upon as proper." In other contexts it is "a statute law made by human beings." All of these meanings stand together under a general notion of *nomos* that refers to the fair and appropriate distribution of power or resources, to the proper share of things being allotted to everyone involved, under whatever circumstances are current. The philosophical argument that the king alone defined *nomos* was a logical extension of the argument that a king could only be a king by surpassing everyone in excellence. Of course, in practice it might be difficult or even impossible to distinguish between a king determining *nomos* on the basis of a philosophically grounded position and a tyrant imposing his will by threats and violence. Anaxarchus took his argument to a higher level, by saying that Zeus as king of the gods had Justice (*Dikē*) and Divine Law (*Themis*) seated beside him as he ruled the universe. He was implying that Alexander was not just the source of society's customs and statute law, but as the son of Zeus/Ammon was also aligned with the forces of right that trumped anything human.

It is not recorded that Alexander made a specific response to Anaxarchus' arguments, but he did recover his equanimity and resume his role as commander-in-chief. Arrian adds, however, that Alexander never denied or excused what he had done. He agreed that he had stumbled, being a human being, and stumbled terribly. That admission did not exclude the notion that he was also a divine being in some unprecedented way; it just meant that he was human at the same time. In this context, it is worth noting that it was in the next year that, according to

Diodorus, Alexander had a son born to him from Barsine, the daughter of a prominent Persian father and a Greek mother (the account of Justin puts the birth two years later). She had first met Alexander long before when her family was living at the court of Philip II in Macedonia, and later she had been married to Memnon, the Greek commander who had presented the biggest threat to Alexander's army when it first crossed over to Asia. She had been captured in 333 and brought along on the expedition: her great beauty had entranced Alexander. The significant point about their child was the name they gave him: Heracles. So far as the surviving evidence shows, this was the first baby ever given that name since the time of the greatest hero of Greek myth. The name became well established in later centuries in the aftermath of Alexander's career, but now it was something radically new. The legendary Heracles had been the child of Zeus and Alcmene, a divine father and a human mother, but it was also said that he simultaneously had Amphitryon, Alcmene's husband, as a human father, too. Whatever Heracles' exact genealogy, he somehow descended from a union of god and human being. The son of Alexander and Barsine carried, for the first time in Greek and Macedonian history, this name that unquestionably identified one of his parents as in some sense divine. That parent was Alexander, and his son's unprecedented name told the world about his status as a being somehow more than human.

Justin

Justin wrote his *Philippic Histories* in Latin perhaps in the third or fourth century AD; we know nothing about him personally. Justin's work was a summary of the much longer work of Pompeius Trogus, a Roman citizen from Gaul in the first century BC. Justin's account of the career of Philip II joins Diodorus' to provide our most detailed evidence for the achievements and goals of Alexander's father. For example, Justin reveals how Philip gained Greek support by showing respect for the gods, especially in waging war to protect the sanctuary of Apollo at Delphi. Justin remarks (8.2) that "Philip alone had risen up to set right the crimes that the combined forces of the world should have punished; therefore, he deserved to be ranked next to the gods, since he had vindicated their majesty." In his account of Philip's amazing transformation of Macedonia from a backwater in the Mediterranean world into an international force, Justin pulls no punches about Philip's aspirations to dominate Greece and his unflinching use of power politics.

§8.

Alexander's vision of his superhuman standing in the world did not make life any more comfortable on the northeastern frontier. Some locals continued to fight for their freedom from his control. The most spectacular resistance formed under the command of Oxyartes, who had taken refuge in a fortress perched atop a precipitous height called the Sogdian Rock. (Its exact location remains undetermined.) From atop the cliffs that they thought made them safe, the defenders mocked the attackers. They shouted down to Alexander that he would have to find "winged soldiers" to get to them. That was of course just the sort of insulting challenge to his honor and superiority that Alexander had never ignored. He called for volunteers from his army with rock-climbing experience, and during the night 300 men equipped with ropes and pitons scaled the snowy rock face at the rear of the fortress. The climb was so dangerous that thirty of them fell to their deaths. On the next morning, Alexander had the news announced to the defenders that they should look behind them to see his "winged soldiers." Astonished at the sight, Oxyartes surrendered immediately. Alexander accepted his submission, and in coming to terms with the barbarian leader he took a step of major significance: now in his late twenties, in (probably) early 327, he married Oxyartes' teenage daughter, Roxane (or Rhoxane). The ages of the bride and groom were in line with Greek expectations for marriage for both sexes. The ancient sources agree that Alexander fell in love with Roxane at first sight; she was said to be the most beautiful woman in Asia (after Darius' wife). It is perfectly plausible that Alexander was enchanted by Roxane, as he appreciated female beauty: he had been attracted to Barsine for that reason, and when he had first seen the royal women captured after the battle of Issus, he had joked with his friends, quoting from a famous story in Herodotus, that these Persians were so lovely that "They hurt your eyes!"

It is clear, too, that Alexander followed not just his heart but also his head in marrying this barbarian princess. The union created an important political alliance with an influential tribal leader in this non-urbanized part of the world. Bactria and Sogdiana, Alexander now knew from hard experience, were regions controlled at the ground level, so to speak, by local chiefs like Oxyartes. They were not governed by a king exercising overall authority who could keep all the locals in line, or by city-states with which it was possible to negotiate political settlements confirmed by sacred oaths. The only way to promote stability and security was to rely on personal ties of loyalty. If Alexander hoped to make it to India without leaving a chaos of rebellion behind him, then he had to arrange stability, and the arrangements had to reflect local realities.

§9.

His arrangement with Oxyartes soon proved its worth. Alexander's army scaled the Sogdian Rock in the spring of 327, in all likelihood. Not long afterwards, he faced an even more formidable challenge: an assault on the mountain redoubt of the Sogdian chieftain Sisimithres (Chorienes). This barbarian leader held the fortifications of the "Rock of Chorienes," a promontory two miles high surrounded by a steep ravine and accessible only by a single narrow path. The Sogdian defenders had gathered a great store of food and were prepared to hold out indefinitely. They believed their fortress to be utterly safe from any human army. Alexander set out to prove them wrong. His engineers worked night and day, piling rocks and trees into the ravine, pinning them in place with stakes pounded into rock to bridge the gap. He stationed his archers and field artillery on the improvised causeway before sending Oxyartes to talk to Sisimithres. Convinced by Oxyartes' description of his friendly relationship with Alexander and having witnessed the Macedonians' tireless and ingenious tactics, Sisimithres surrendered. Alexander made him an ally, too. The supplies in the Sogdian's fortress were so vast that during two months of winter weather so severe that Alexander's army risked starvation, his soldiers dined well on gifts from their new friends. According to Greek and Macedonian codes of honor, a superior given a gift owed an even greater one in return. Alexander accordingly presented Sisimithres with 30,000 head of cattle that he captured in a campaign in the summer of 327 against the Sacae. This Scythian tribe had either betrayed a treaty with Alexander, or had simply been an easy target for plunder in this country that could not be conquered or administered like Greece or Persia. Persian kings had regarded Sogdians, or at least some of them, as their subjects, but their control of this farthest frontier of the empire had always been superficial at best. Even Alexander could alter that reality only so much.

8

VICTORY AND
FRUSTRATION IN INDIA
(327 TO 326 BC)

§ 1.

After Alexander killed Cleitus, things got worse: his Macedonians and Greeks were increasingly hostile to the changes he made. It galled them to see barbarians, defeated barbarians, sitting on seats of power and basking in the king's favor. Tension grew when Alexander attempted another innovation in the protocol at court. The new step was to expand the use of the Persian custom of prostration; this decision perhaps reflected Alexander's growing sense of his own nature, mixing the human and the divine. In observing this custom, Persians were not worshipping a king as a god. Their religion saw the Great King as an earthly agent of the god Ahura Mazda, but the agent was not himself divine. Greeks saw this custom differently. For them prostration was a posture of adoration and worship practiced in the temples of the gods, before the statues of divinities; it served as a concrete sign in the human world recognizing the deities' supernatural existence. If Macedonians or Greeks prostrated themselves before Alexander, they would have been implying, at the very least, that their leader was more than human.

In the months after Cleitus' murder, Alexander conducted an experiment to see if prostration could be accepted as normal protocol in his court, at least when non-Europeans were present in the audience. He discussed his plan ahead of time with a select group of Macedonians and Greeks in his inner circle. They agreed to observe the custom at a carefully orchestrated occasion. Alexander purposely did not order non-Persians to prostrate themselves before him; they would voluntarily follow the lead of his inner circle. The historian Callisthenes was one of those who promised to set the example, as was the philosopher Anaxarchus.

On the chosen evening, at a dinner hosting Macedonians, Greeks, and Persians, Anaxarchus brought up the topic of divinity. He argued that Alexander deserved to be recognized as a human being who has achieved divine status, and that Alexander was more deserving of this even than Dionysus and Heracles. Alexander was "going beyond" even their great expeditions, and he had earned his divine status already, before his death.

Callisthenes vehemently rejected Anaxarchus' argument. He was perhaps surprised by the bluntness of the philosopher's words, and he was certainly still smarting from his failure – and Anaxarchus' success – in the effort to bring Alexander back to his senses after the death of Cleitus. Echoing the views of his uncle Aristotle on barbarians, Callisthenes directly rebuked Alexander for having lost sight of the proper goal of his expedition: to subjugate barbarian Asia to Greek rule. Alexander was extremely angry but did not reply. Instead, he moved on to the next stage of his scheme. As planned, he passed around a gold cup filled with wine. The Macedonians and Greeks who were party to the plan each took the cup, drained it, and then prostrated themselves before the king. Rising from the floor, each then stepped to Alexander's side. He greeted them with a kiss, a gesture with a long history in both Greek and Persian culture to demonstrate respectful attachment to another person (and not, in this context, erotic love). One after another they went through this process, until it was Callisthenes' turn. He skipped the prostration. Alexander was deep in conversation with someone else – he was doing all he could to hide that a scripted performance was taking place – and missed the omission. When it was pointed out to him, he refused to kiss Callisthenes. The haughty historian left the party exclaiming, "Well, I'll just go away poorer by one kiss." The Persians then stepped in, one by one, to keep the prostrations going, but Leonnatus, an especially prominent commander and member of the Macedonian social elite, mocked them in front of Alexander. It was clearly too late now for the experiment to succeed. Alexander never repeated it. He had learned that some people, even those close to him and whose cooperation he needed (for now), were never going to align themselves with his new approach to culture and rule. Like Aristotle and Callisthenes, they were always going to see the world as defined by a cultural division between superior Greeks and inferior barbarians.

§2.

Alexander took this bitter lesson to heart. It was probably at this time in 327 that he arranged for 30,000 young men back in Persia to be picked out to learn to speak Greek and to fight as soldiers with Macedonian weapons. He told them that, if they succeeded in their training, he would name their unit his "Successors." He did not tell his Macedonian army of this plan. A force of 30,000 new Persian troops was almost as large – and as expensive – as the army of Macedonians and Greeks with which he had first left Europe to conquer Asia. Alexander kept to himself what he intended to do with this new Iranian army-in-training, but surely he was spending the money to create a source of loyal support for himself that would, through its specific education, be trained in the "mixed customs" that he saw as integral to his future plans.

The loyalty that had seen Alexander's army through countless battles was no longer certain, even among those closest to the king. He could no longer count on his men. Further proof that his relationship with his men had changed forever came in the so-called "Pages' Conspiracy." Pages were young men from the high reaches of Macedonian society chosen to serve the king as a special group of attendants. They had access to his presence and functioned as trusted, if junior, members of his inner circle. They were allowed to handle lethal weapons in the king's presence and went with him on his outings to hunt wild animals, a regular Macedonian and Greek activity for exercise and male social bonding that Alexander frequently organized during his expedition. On one of these hunts, a page outraged the strict rules of hierarchy in the group by spearing a wild boar before the king could strike it. The expected punishment for this failure in self-control was a whipping, and that is what Alexander ordered for the rule breaker. The young hothead became so angry about his painful humiliation that he formed a conspiracy with eight other pages to assassinate Alexander. One of the plotters lost his nerve, however, and revealed the murder plan. Alexander rewarded the informer lavishly, and those he named were condemned to death by stoning, the Macedonian penalty for regicide. Both Arrian and Curtius portray the accused pages as giving speeches at their trial that vented their anger at Alexander's policy toward barbarians and his violence toward the Macedonians who opposed his initiative. Even if, as seems likely, their plot was actually fueled by personal feelings, they believed that they could win sympathy from the rank-and-file by decrying Alexander's policies.

§3.

The sources disagree on whether Callisthenes had actively encouraged the pages to kill their king or knew of the plot. But he was actively involved in educating the young men, and Alexander blamed him. He was arrested, dying sometime later, and we have no clear account of his death, whether by illness or by execution. Some scholars suggest that Alexander intended for Callisthenes, a Greek, to stand trial before the Greek alliance, of which Alexander was still hegemon. It seems equally plausible, however, that Alexander refrained from killing him immediately, either because he was unsure about Callisthenes' role in the Pages' Conspiracy, or simply because the historian was Aristotle's relative.

These details do not matter nearly as much as the obvious fact: on the eve of Alexander's departure toward India, his court was riven by suspicion, intrigue, and anger. Alexander could not uniformly trust his commanders or the men he commanded. They had been in Bactria and on edge too long; they lacked their commander's vision and his unbreakable perseverance toward his goals. His best hope in motivating them was for action, movement, victory and all its benefits, material and psychological.

§4.

India was the key. Alexander had read in Herodotus that the parts of the world farthest from Greece offered "the finest things" and that India in particular held an immense amount of gold. As ever, Alexander worked to ensure security behind him and to secure intelligence about what was ahead. He stationed a trusted commander, a Macedonian with 10,000 infantry and 3,000 cavalry, in Bactria, and he reinforced the city of Alexandria in the Hindu Kush range with a mixed contingent of locals and older veterans from his own army. In the mountainous region of the Paropamisadans he placed a Persian commander. He had sent scouts ahead into northwestern India (as the Greeks called the region east of the mountains; today it is in the country of Pakistan). The rulers there were alerted to his approach and came out to meet him as he approached the high passes to their country. Alexander learned from these local rulers that the region was torn by conflict; the men who came to meet him were looking for his support against their enemies. Of these, the most prominent Indian was Taxiles (Ambhi). Taxiles ruled territory between the Indus River on the west and the Hydaspes (Jhelum) River on the east.

Taxiles and the other Indian rulers then led half of Alexander's army, commanded by Hephaestion and Perdiccas, with the heaviest equipment, over the Khyber Pass to the Indus River. They had orders to wait there for Alexander and the rest of the army to find a way across the river. Alexander took a more northern route with the balance of the army. They fought their way forward, defeating those tribes who refused to surrender.

These victories were incredibly profitable. His army captured 40,000 Indians, who could be hired as servants or sold as slaves, and a quarter of a million head of fine cattle. Always thirsty for knowledge, and with no limits to the scope of his curiosity, Alexander inspected the captured cows to identify the best ones; these he sent back to Macedonia as breeding animals for the improvement of European livestock. Alexander's vision of a new and integrated world was not limited to a blending of human cultures. His approach to conquest had not softened, either. Here he put to death 7,000 Indian mercenaries who held out for three days after his army surrounded them. Diodorus claims that Alexander had promised to let them go if they surrendered but broke his word. Arrian says that the mercenaries had promised to enlist with Alexander, but broke their word and tried to flee; death was their penalty for disloyalty. In the face of ancient sources that directly contradict each other, we have to rely on an understanding of Alexander's character at this point.

§ 5.

Biographers are always in danger of arguing in circles. If the story of Alexander is the story of an irrational killer, as some modern scholars imagine, then the ancient author who sees this mass execution as an unmotivated act of violence will seem more consistent and reliable. If the story of Alexander is the story of a man obsessed with loyalty and courage, whose most violent actions were always in response to betrayal or cowardice, then Arrian's account is more plausible. If Alexander's life is the story of a man whose character changed, through hardships and repeated treachery by those close to him, then it becomes much harder to weigh these two accounts. Perhaps it makes sense to look at Alexander in court as opposed to Alexander on the march. It was during periods of delay – winter camps, affairs of state – that the most morally questionable acts of mistrust, violence, and destruction seem to have occurred: the burning of the palace at Persepolis, the murder of Cleitus. On the march, Alexander seems consistently in control, dispensing mercy and harshness according to tactical and strategic aims, seeking advantage for his army and for his plans, with little thought to personal safety or concerns unrelated to victory, security, and excellence. In that light, the costly execution of 7,000 potential slaves, and the loss of that amount of wealth that he could have gifted to his soldiers, would seem senseless except as the price for a public demonstration of the perils of treachery, a lesson to other Indian tribes whose paths might cross his.

Whatever changes the difficult years had worked on Alexander's character or behavior, his longing, his *pothos*, to "go beyond" remained overwhelming. His route toward the Indus brought him to a place his scouts had identified: the town called Nysa, whose residents worshipped a god that could only, it seemed to Alexander, be Dionysus. At Nysa alone, of all parts of that region, ivy grew, the plant sacred to Dionysus. Alexander paused on his march to visit all the sites in the region that he could identify with Dionysus, showing his respect for the god by granting the locals their independence. He wanted everyone to remember that he had been here – Nysa was the farthest extent of Dionysus' journey east – and he wanted everyone to know that where the god had stopped, Alexander had also stopped, but that Alexander had then gone beyond.

§6.

In the second half of the year 327, Alexander's *pothos* brought him to a vertiginous ridge of stone that leapt 5,000 feet from its base on the Indus River. This was the Rock of Aornus ("The Rock So Tall that No Bird Can Fly that High"). A defiant band of locals had fortified themselves on the top of this promontory. Alexander set his engineers to constructing a causeway across a ravine – a mile wide and 600 feet deep – so that his artillery could suppress the defenders while his infantry attacked. The causeway was complete in three days. Amazed and dismayed at the speed and energy of Alexander's attack, the barbarians surrendered. Alexander had put everything he had into this spectacular victory, moved by a desire to outdo his ancestor Heracles. Myth had it that Heracles, the most famous Greek hero, had failed to capture the Rock of Aornus. The mountain fortress was neither tactically nor strategically significant, but it earned a place on Alexander's itinerary, as Nysa had earned one, as an occasion to demonstrate excellence that surpassed the achievements even of conquering gods.

§7.

In 326 Alexander moved forward to Taxila. When he arrived, he assembled a group of Indian religious sages with a special reputation for wisdom. These belonged to the most striking type of holy men in India, the kind that Greeks called "Naked Wise Men" because they wore little or no clothing. Like other ascetics in India, these men lived with extreme self-discipline, shunning the conventions of ordinary existence, from regular meals to sex. Some of the Indian ascetics had openly opposed Alexander's move into their homeland. The king was therefore both suspicious of them and curious about their intellectual abilities.

Alexander put these men to a test; its nature reflected his curiosity, and the stakes aimed to make a point. He would ask them questions meant to be impossible to answer. He would kill first the one giving the worst answer. The questions would probe their wisdom and wit, and the threatened punishment would put these renowned sages – who had presumed to criticize Alexander's mission of conquest – to the same test Alexander faced every hour of his life. In his relentless pursuit of excellence, after all, he was engaged in a perpetual contest of wisdom with the whole world. As he had always known, but as recent events had shown so clearly, his own life was forfeit at any moment, should he fail any of the daily tests before him. He wanted these Indian sages to prove their reputations under the same circumstances.

The story of "Alexander and the Naked Sages" became a popular one later, retold in many ways, with differing details. The heart of what happened seems to be a version of a classic logic puzzle, and we recount it here accordingly. At first Alexander posed questions about the nature of the world, but then he switched to queries about how to live. He asked how someone could be most loved; "If he is the best and most powerful (*kratistos*, the most *krateros*) but not a terror," came the reply. And then, "How can someone from the human race become a god?" The sage whose turn it was said, "If that person accomplishes what a human being cannot accomplish." Next, the king asked whether life or death was stronger; "Life," was the reply, "that endures so many bad things." The last question was, "Up to what point is it a good thing for a man to live?" Each man answered in turn, and the final response was, "Until he doesn't think dying is better than living." Faced with these brilliantly paradoxical answers to what he had designed to be confounding questions, Alexander then asked the last and oldest of the wise men to judge his colleagues' performance.

The old man answered, "Each of us has answered worse than the one before." Alexander responded, "In that case, you will die first for giving that judgment." The sage boldly reproached him: "Not at any rate, king, if you weren't lying when you said you'd put to death the one who answered worst." The elderly wise man had deftly outwitted the conqueror with a logic puzzle known as "the liar's paradox": If his own answer was "worst" by being incorrect, then one of the previous sages must have answered worse than he had, and would deserve to die first. If his own answer was "worst," then it must be correct, and he therefore did not deserve to die.

Honorably honest, Alexander had to acknowledge the old man's cleverness and freedom of speech under pressure: he sent all the sages away alive, with gifts. They had bested him in the contest, and he rewarded their victory – even if he knew that such plain-living men had no use for material goods! Alexander was clearly impressed by this episode, and he persuaded another ascetic sage named Calanus to join him on the expedition, aiming to learn as much as he could of this Indian wisdom so potent it could beat him in an intellectual battle.

§8.

In May 326, Alexander learned that he faced battle with another potent Indian enemy, a military one that awaited him on the far bank of the Hydaspes River. The opponent was Porus, king of the region beyond the river and an enemy of Taxiles. Porus was determined to keep Alexander from proceeding any further east into the Indian subcontinent, and he had the resources to do it. His army was large, and the 200 war elephants he deployed made crossing the river to attack him seemingly impossible. Alexander's forces would have to be transported across the water on boats and rafts, and the overpowering scent of so many elephants would make the horses go wild as soon as they smelled it. Without cavalry, Alexander had no chance to overcome Porus. He had to get across the river with enough combined arms to win a battle against a powerful foe. He chose to wear away his enemy's patience. Again and again, he ordered small forces to approach the western bank of the river. Each time Porus expected that the Macedonians were launching their cross-river invasion and arrayed his forces to defend. Each time the Macedonians melted back to camp. Eventually, Porus had to spare his men the rigors of mustering at arms, and the Indian satisfied himself with stationing sentries along the riverbank. These would report back when the true invasion was imminent; it would take a long time to transport an army across the river, after all, and the Indian soldiers and their elephants would have plenty of warning.

Alexander, meanwhile, took a combined force of infantry and cavalry – 11,000 men – upriver 17 miles north, to a spot where an island split the river. The crossing would be easier here, and the island would hide his efforts from view. The bulk of his army remained downstream, facing Porus. The plan was for the upriver force to cross and launch a flanking attack against Porus; at the same time, the main army would force a crossing of the Hydaspes. On the night of the crossing the sky was wild with thunder, lightning, and rain. The upriver forces delayed their crossing until dawn and clear weather. In the light of day, Porus' scouts soon spotted the Macedonian flotilla and rushed back to alert Porus. When Alexander's boats struck against the shore, his men poured forth, only to discover that they were not yet on the opposite shore but only as far as the island. Only barely were they able to ford the second branch of the river, in a place just shallow enough for men and horses to cross without drowning. They assembled before any opposition arrived, and Alexander advanced with his cavalry in front, his infantry behind, and his mounted archers able to provide covering fire. Porus was torn. Was this attack sweeping down from the north the main thrust of the Macedonian advance? Or yet another diversion? He took a chance, made his decision, and sent his son north with a limited blocking force of cavalry and chariots. His gamble failed. Alexander captured every chariot and killed one in five of the horsemen, including the son of Porus.

Alexander still had to overcome the massive force of elephants at the center of the Indian line. So, he moved what appeared to be all of his cavalry to the right of the line; this was intended to draw the Indian cavalry in that direction. He kept one unit from view, and when the Indian army attacked toward Alexander's right, where he seemed strongest, this hidden squadron charged Porus' cavalry in its rear. Forced to fight in two directions, the Indian horsemen retreated to the safety of the elephants. Knowing he could not expect European and Persian horses to face elephants, Alexander sent his infantry against the now-crowded formation of Indian cavalry, infantry, and elephants closely packed in a milling throng. At first the elephants did savage damage and the Indians fought hard. But when the beasts received wounds, they began doing as much damage to their own lines as to the enemy. In the ensuing rout more than 20,000 Indians died. Porus never stopped fighting, even after he was seriously wounded atop his elephant. His courage was indomitable. When Alexander sent Taxiles to ask for his surrender, Porus nearly killed him; finally, Alexander sent an old friend of the Indian king, who had been treated well by Alexander. Porus laid down his arms, and Alexander went to meet his bloodied foe.

War Elephants

Persian and Indian armies placed their trained elephants in the center of their battle lines, where they could spearhead a charge, block an opponent's attack, or provide protection for foot soldiers. The beasts had their greatest effect by producing panic among the enemy's cavalry horses or infantry through their towering height and bulk, the thunderous noise of their trumpeting as they charged shaking the ground, and, for horses confronting elephants for the first time, their frightening smell. Commanders could send elephants to stomp into the opposing ranks, trampling men with their feet, spearing them with their tusks, and picking them up with their trunks to crash them to the ground.

Even trained elephants, however, could react unpredictably under battle conditions. Despite their thick skins, they could be wounded by arrows or spears. The soles of their feet were tender and susceptible to bruising when they pounded across the field. Wounded elephants were impossible to control, often throwing their own lines into confusion or even killing those on their side as they bulled their way off the battlefield.

The encounter between the Indian and the Macedonian became one of the most famous moments of Alexander's career. He asked Porus, "How should you be treated?" Porus answered, "As a king should." Alexander, wishing to recognize his opponent's great courage, then said, "But what do you want for yourself?" Porus responded that his previous answer said all that needed to be said. Admiring his foe's calm dignity, Alexander not only kept Porus as king of the region east of the river but added territory to his command. If Taxiles had hoped that Alexander would get rid of Porus for him, he was underestimating the Macedonian's admiration for valor and his astuteness in keeping effective rulers in place when he trusted their sense of honor.

§9.

Alexander saw his victory over Porus as a turning point in the history of the world, and he left clear and tangible evidence of this. He ordered large silver medallions minted to commemorate the battle: on one side these coin-like tokens depicted the Indian forces that Alexander had faced and overcome, four-horse chariots or archers with enormous bows; on the other was Alexander on horseback confronting Porus astride his massive elephant. The mounted figure of Alexander was brandishing a thunderbolt in his hand while receiving a crown from Nikē, the goddess of victory. This scene made an unmistakable claim: Alexander was the son of Zeus and he commanded his father's divine power (so much on display on the night of his river-crossing). Around this time Alexander also had minted smaller gold pieces that made an even more striking statement. On one side of these was an Indian elephant; the other was filled with the king's portrait in profile, wearing an aegis, the shirt covered in scales and snakes' heads that the goddess Athena wore in her role as divinity of war, and a headdress made of an elephant's skull. From Alexander' temples curled the horns of a ram, the symbols of Ammon, the Egyptian Zeus.

Never before had any living Macedonian or Greek been depicted on such objects. Never before had a living human being been shown on a public document with attributes marking him as superhuman, as sharing in divinity. Like the name Heracles that Alexander had given his son by Barsine, these images proclaimed to the world that a new era had arrived. The Indian sage had said that when a "person accomplishes what a human being cannot accomplish," he would become a god. When Alexander stood on the east bank of the Hydaspes River, he claimed the dawn of an epoch when this had happened. He had "gone beyond" the nature and status of a man. The story of Alexander's life requires that we understand this statement as well as we can, living as we do in a time and place that dismisses the idea of any living being walking the earth bearing the mixed natures of the human and the divine, or at best confines that possibility to a short period of time 2,000 years ago.

§10.

Alexander's vision propelled him forward; leisure was not for superhuman beings. The mere mortals in his army did require rest, however, and Alexander waited a month before resuming the march deeper into India, toward whatever lay beyond. Since it was impossible to know which direction would lead around the world, he ordered a fleet of boats to be built for sailing down the Indus River to the outer ocean, in case that turned out to be the best way to go in pursuit of his geographical goal. He then led the army to a series of victories east of the Hydaspes River. The battles were hard, as many of the Indian settlements resisted to the death. The campaign wore on the Macedonians. The bloody fighting was a strain, but they were used to fighting; what they had never experienced before was the monsoon, the wearing combination of high temperatures and humidity through seventy consecutive days of heavy rains.

The rain finally broke this undefeated army. Encamped on the west bank of the Hyphasis (Beas) River, the troops looked across the water with dread at the seemingly endless regions beyond, which their scouts reported were defended by large Indian armies, fielding even more elephants than Porus had. Soldiers clustered in spontaneous assemblies, the majority declaring they would march no farther, mutiny if necessary. When Alexander heard, he assembled his commanders to give an impassioned speech. Arrian reports that the king said he would either persuade them or be persuaded by them. He reminded them of their victories, all the lands they had conquered and put under Macedonian rule. He bluntly stated his personal creed: there was no limit to the work of a man who was *gennaios*. This Greek term is usually translated "noble," but that fails to express the depth of its meaning for Alexander; even if Arrian rewrote the wording of the speech for his history, it captured Alexander's ethos brilliantly. Aristotle said that a man was *gennaios* who "is not separated from his own nature," a concept that we might rephrase as "remaining authentic," or "preserving personal authenticity." This sense helps us understand what Alexander meant, but what helps more is to see the word in the Homeric *Iliad*, the piece of literature that, more than any other, informed Alexander's view of himself. *Gennaios* occurs only once in the poem (5.253), in a context that fits Alexander's situation on the bank of the Hyphasis. When the Greek hero Diomedes is about to fight not one but two top-flight Trojan heroes, a fellow soldier urges him to turn back in the face of this overwhelming danger to his life. Diomedes replies, "Don't talk to me about retreat; you won't persuade me. A *gennaios* man as I am does not shrink from fighting ... the goddess Pallas Athena does not allow me to run away." As Aristotle taught him to do, Alexander looked to Homer as the ultimate guide to achieving the excellence that gave his life meaning; at this moment of crisis, he called on a concept of excellence from the *Iliad*. It demanded that he, like Diomedes, reject any argument for turning back, no matter how great the danger and no matter how many others wanted to quit. Alexander went on to remind his men of Heracles, how his achievements had transformed him into a god, and how they had already, together, surpassed both Heracles and Dionysus in their expedition.

A long silence followed Alexander's speech. Finally, after he encouraged the generals to speak up, one of them haltingly began by saying that he took Alexander at his word that this was an occasion for persuasion, not compulsion. In short, he told the king that the mass of the army had lost heart and would not go on willingly; if they were forced to go, they would be unreliable in battle. The other officers began weeping when their comrade finished. Alexander, angry and disgusted, dismissed the meeting. The next day he announced that he would go on with anyone willing to follow him; he would force no one to accompany him. Like Achilles in the *Iliad*, his sense of honor betrayed, he then shut himself away in his tent, refusing even his Companions. He stayed away from the army for three days, hoping the soldiers would change their minds. They did not. Alexander had sacrifices performed, to test the will of the gods. The sacrifices produced bad omens for the river crossing and the journey beyond. With this, Alexander relented and turned his army around. Before departing, he had twelve immense towers constructed on the riverbank commemorating the support he had received from each of the gods of Olympus. Still, it seems impossible to overestimate his disappointment when he finally turned his face from gazing east for the last time. But not even a superhuman king could lead an all-too-human army that lacked the dedication to demonstrating an excellence going beyond that of all others, the commitment that for Alexander was as necessary as breathing. For Alexander, the only acceptable definition of life was the repeated credo of the *Iliad*: "always be the best, be superior to others" (6.208 and elsewhere).

Some scholars believe that Alexander arranged for the sacrifices to fail, as a face-saving excuse for changing his mind. No ancient source suggests this. On the edge of the world, the king was minting coins asserting his own divinity; in his tent with his hardened veteran commanders, he invoked Heracles and Dionysus. The story of Alexander's life is marked by respect for the gods. Even his competition with divinity, his efforts to surpass his ancestor Heracles, was a mark of deep piety. As a child, when asked why he did not compete at the Olympic Games, he said "I will, when I can compete only against kings." The man who competed with gods did so because he honored the gods. This was not a man to fabricate signs from the gods as a cynical mask for his own wounded pride.

§11.

At the Indus River he found construction on his fleet going strong; by the late fall of 326 it numbered 800 sizable boats supplemented by countless smaller craft. He embarked some troops and horses on these transports and deployed the bulk of the army, including the war elephants now in his force, on both sides of the river to march alongside the fleet. He was going to proceed south down the Indus to Ocean (on the border of the continents in Greek geography), sweeping aside any opposition in his path.

And opposition there was. Some locals came over to his side, joining his allies from the northwestern regions of India, but others, led by the militarily strong Malli and urged on by the Indian philosophers known as Brahmans, united to resist him. Alexander devised a pincer movement to take them on multiple fronts. To launch a surprise attack on the enemy, Alexander himself led a picked force through fifty miles of desert in twenty-four hours. His tactics succeeded, and thousands of Indians were killed. So fierce was their dedication to their freedom that some of them burned their houses down with themselves inside rather than surrender. After days of hard fighting, Alexander's men began to lose their enthusiasm and initiative, which of course made their leader furious. When it came time to attack the walled citadel of a Malli town, Alexander was the first up the siege ladder. He had just stepped off onto the wall with three others when the ladder broke under the weight of the men following him. To the horror of his troops, he leaped down inside the wall to face the defenders by himself. The other three jumped after him. The Indians showered them with arrows, immediately killing one of the Macedonians and seriously wounding Alexander with a shot that pierced his chest. The other two soldiers protected him by holding over his body the shield that he had taken from the sanctuary of Athena at Troy eight years before and always had carried with him in combat. His troops outside broke through the wall in a frenzy to rescue him. He was carried out on his shield passing in and out of consciousness. When the arrow was cut out of his body, he passed out from the pain, but the bleeding stopped. His life was saved, barely.

What the army heard, however, was that their leader had been killed. The troops fell into instant despair, bewailing their fate, leaderless and such an unimaginable distance from home. Their joy was ecstatic when Alexander was carried into camp lying on a stretcher and raised his arm to them. In a supreme act of will, he stood up, mounted his horse, rode to his tent, and walked a few steps, almost dead from loss of blood. The men flocked around him throwing flowers, eager to touch him to prove to themselves that he lived. Some of Alexander's friends angered him by blaming him for having risked his life, but a gruff old Greek soldier spoke up to say, "Alexander, this is what men do." The veteran then quoted a line of poetry from Greek drama saying that suffering is obligatory for the man who accomplishes something. This reference pleased Alexander to no end, and from then on he valued the old man highly. Acting on the army's renewed enthusiasm, Alexander pushed on. The Malli and some others, awed by Alexander's courage, stopped their resistance and were made allies with territories to control, but other Indians fought on with a ferocity matched only by Alexander's lethal treatment of all who opposed him. Tens of thousands were killed in his advance to the delta of the Indus River where it flowed into the Indian Ocean. Some modern scholars judge this violence to be mindless slaughter perpetrated by a terrorist, the pathological outpouring of Alexander's frustration at the failure of his plan to march as far eastward as the world allowed. The rejoinder to this interpretation is that Alexander was continuing the policy that he had consistently followed from the beginning: destroy those who opposed him, reward those who joined him. It is normal and indeed inevitable (recent experiments in behavioral psychology teach us) to try to make ethical distinctions based on numbers, to say that the killing of a few is "practical power politics" but the killing of many is "terrorism." Modern judgments aside, whether few or many died, Alexander, generous and pitiless by turns, was consistent in his policy.

9

RETURNING TO BABYLON AND BECOMING DIVINE (326 TO 323 BC)

§ 1.

Alexander had dreamed of surpassing Dionysus and Heracles by continuing into the unexplored (by Greeks) east until he had encircled the world. Now he had turned away from the dream. The pain of this failure was vivid. Still, he marched south along the Indus River, reaching one extreme limit of the terrestrial world at Pattala at the upper end of the Indus Delta. Pattala's inhabitants had fled, but Alexander persuaded them to return to their town and help him defend it against neighboring tribes. He ordered construction of a harbor and a fortified citadel and wells and irrigation in the countryside to support more productive farming. Alexander was governing the strip of India that he covered, following his vision of empire. He relied more than ever on local leaders, while also still placing Macedonians in positions of command. His most important Indian ally was Porus, and Alexander worked to strengthen this former opponent's rule, to extend his territory, and to ensure his ability to govern as a loyal and powerful ally.

While navigating his way through the confusing tangle of waterways of the delta running to the Indian Ocean, Alexander lost several ships in the treacherous currents and tides. At the edge of the sub-continent, he performed the sacrifices that Ammon in Egypt had prescribed to mark his success on reaching

Ocean. He then sailed out to sea and sacrificed to Poseidon, the god of the seas, just as he had done ten years earlier when crossing the Hellespont into Asia. He poured an offering of wine into the water and threw in the golden cup after it, praying that the god grant his fleet a safe return to Mesopotamia. He returned to the delta and ordered a second harbor constructed, the infrastructure for sustained commerce by sea between India and his empire to the west. He wanted travelers and merchants to have an alternative to the laborious and expensive overland trip.

§ 2.

This east-west journey presented difficult challenges because the route was long and wholly underdeveloped. The coast from India to Mesopotamia was a barren expanse offering little food and almost no water. Alexander's army would march back along this route, skirting the sea and escorted by his fleet, but his ships would be hard-pressed to carry sufficient supplies to support their crews' four-month return journey. Alexander therefore split his force, as he had often done earlier on his eastern march, and sent a portion of his army – including the biggest eaters of all, his war elephants – back by the northern route, under the command of Craterus. He himself characteristically chose the harder challenge, the land route, dispatching caches of supplies to be pre-positioned along the coast. This daring plan, to supply a naval fleet by a land force marching overland, reversed the usual supply arrangements for giant armies and was unimaginably audacious and risky. The harsh country and its warlike tribes were as threatening as any enemy Alexander had ever faced. Semiramis, the legendary Assyrian warrior queen, had completed this march, barely, emerging from the ordeal with only twenty survivors out of her entire army. Cyrus, the great Persian king, had tried to invade India by this route as well, and of his army only seven men survived the ordeal. Alexander chose this march, not in spite of these tales of disaster, but because of them. If he could not surpass the gods by crossing India, he could surpass the great rulers of the past on a road west.

He laid his plans carefully, as always. Nearchus would command the fleet, with instructions to conduct a detailed survey of the coastal lands they passed. Alexander wanted charts of all existing and possible harbors, and all towns; he wanted to know about agriculture in the region; he wanted knowledge, both for its own sake and to help him reshape the world. A trickle of commerce between southwestern Asia and the Mediterranean lands was centuries old, but Alexander's work now would in later times create a steady flow, despite the hardships and dangers of sea travel, that would change the face of the ancient world.

Our sources differ wildly when they report the size of the army that marched with Alexander along the coast. One estimate counts 30,000 troops, followed by innumerable independent traders, women, and children (the camp followers). So long as the army stayed close to the coast, the new region provided sufficient food and water. The research scientists whom Alexander had long ago commissioned to accompany him kept busy collecting specimens of plants and animals that they had never seen, and the more commercially minded of the expedition gathered quantities of valuable myrrh and other rare botanicals.

The army faced armed resistance all along its route. The greatest threat came from the Oreitai, but their strength lay largely in a web of alliances, which collapsed in the face of the Macedonian army. They prudently surrendered. As was his usual procedure, Alexander accepted the suppliants into an alliance. He ordered their largest village to be expanded into a city, to take advantage of what he saw as its favorable location for growth. He appointed a satrap to govern the region, with orders to collect provisions for the fleet, and then moved westward into the even harsher desert of Gedrosia.

§3.

Here conditions changed drastically for the worse, as a range of mountains forced the army away from the coast. Food and water became scarcer. What little the scouts found had to provision both the army and the fleet, and the distance between the two grew ever wider. The army suffered under the heat, which reached 120 degrees Fahrenheit. They marched at night and rested through the broiling heat of the day, but they still had to forage for water under the relentless sun. They killed their pack animals for meat. The deep sand clutched at their wheeled carts, and the sick and injured had to be left behind, a horrible shock to them and to the comrades forced to abandon them. Dehydration saps both mind and body, and Alexander's men and animals became crazed with thirst and suffering. The forces of nature then mocked Alexander's best planning with a terribly ironic vengeance. A sudden torrential shower in the hills above the army's encampment sent a terrestrial tsunami of floodwater down a ravine and into their unsuspecting midst. Soldiers who had gone to sleep parched with thirst woke to find themselves drowning in a muddy torrent. Men died by the hundreds, and the expedition lost irreplaceable arms and equipment. The camp followers, who had overnighted in a gully, were swept away in a contorted mass of corpses.

Alexander endured this, and everything else his army suffered. In battle he always led from the front, setting an example by putting his own body in the path of the gravest dangers, defying injury and death to instill courage in his men. He did the same now, with a gesture that would become famous. When a scout brought the king a helmet filled with water, Alexander took it before the eyes of his army and poured it onto the sand without taking a sip. The enemy was thirst, as piercing as any Persian spear; the scout had brought comfort and healing to the king's hand. When he threw it away, the message was clear: Alexander could defeat this enemy. As Arrian tells the story, it was as if Alexander had provided a drink for every man in the army.

§4.

Once the army found a route closer to the shore, Alexander personally led probes to discover springs of water. After two months, in the fall of 325, the survivors emerged from the west-ern frontier of the Gedrosian Desert and into fertile lands that could support life. The march had been very costly in men and treasure. Not even Alexander's strong leadership and advanced planning had prevented the tragedies of the march, of which the most horrible was leaving behind their comrades to die alone. Alexander was distraught. He turned his anger against the region's satraps, condemning them for failing to send him the supplies he had ordered. Plutarch reports that Alexander executed one of them with his own hands, skewering the incom-petent subordinate with his spear.

The march through the Gedrosian Desert was a disaster – there is no other way to see it – and scholars have long debated how we should understand it. The most critical view holds that Alexander, angry at his army's refusal to continue eastward across India, intentionally set out on an arduous journey to punish his men. This makes little sense. Alexander took only part of the army with him along the coast, and there is no evidence that he selected these troops for especially lethal duty. The men who marched the desert with Alexander certainly do not seem to have been selected for disloyalty; on the contrary, for them to have held together under these circumstances suggests they were dedicated to their commander, no matter how risky his plans. Also unpersuasive is the opinion that Alexander blamed the satraps in order to exonerate himself and push responsibility onto their shoulders. This army, having marched and fought together for so long, was unlikely to be deceived or confused at any point regarding who was responsible for what; they knew what successes and failures belonged to their king, to his officers and imperial administrators, and to themselves.

It seems most plausible to understand this hellish trial as yet another contest, one that Alexander identified and entered freely, driven by his abiding desire always to "go beyond." In this agony, as in every contest of Alexander's adult life, the opponents and the audience did not consist of his officers or his army. Alexander competed with kings, with ancient heroes, with himself, and, increasingly, with gods. He had gone farther than Dionysus and Heracles (although not as far as he wished), and now on his road home he tried to "go beyond" Semiramis, the great Cyrus, the deadly sands of Gedrosia, and the divine forces of nature by punching a viable route across the barren landscape desert and thereby establish a viable route for trade – and Alexander's vision of civilization across space. The prize was valued at its cost. Alexander emerged with more than a handful of men and so could claim victory. The price was extremely high – the king might see himself as superhuman, but he could not in the final analysis control nature at every turn, those powers being the domain of only a select few of the gods. There was no hiding the price, and only Alexander could know if the victory of survival and endurance was worth it.

§5.

Alexander had been gone from the western lands of his empire for a long time, having left his decentralized system in the hands of nearly autonomous and hugely powerful regional governors. Each of these he had selected for loyalty – the virtue he prized above all others – but these all-too-human men were susceptible to temptation and corruption by the unimaginable power and riches that their positions carried. With their king, and accountability, far away, many of the governors and satraps succumbed to their worst impulses. When Alexander reached Carmania (in southeastern Iran), he summoned those officials who had been accused by the locals of various crimes: inflicting arbitrary punishments, robbing temples, and enrolling mercenaries to serve as the enforcers for their crimes. These disloyal minions were Macedonians and Greeks; most of the Persian satraps had remained true to their ruler (though those who had not were also brought to justice). Alexander executed the criminals along with hundreds of their followers. The severity of the punishment fit the gravity of the crimes. Locals mistreated could become the agents of violent rebellion, such as the one Alexander had just suppressed in the satrapy of Drangiana. Sanctuaries plundered were sites of sacrilege guaranteed to call down the wrath of the gods. Mercenary armies were direct threats to the power and authority of the king. Even in this far-reaching empire, there could be only one army answering to only one man. Arrian reports that Alexander did nothing more effective for preserving loyalty among the subjects of his empire than this clear demonstration that abusive officials would face justice, regardless of their position or nationality.

Craterus now arrived with the force he had led back from India, and Alexander in joy treated his long-suffering troops to a week of relaxation filled with athletic and musical contests, sacrifices, and drinking parties. Some sources describe the celebrations as literal bacchanals, with drunken revels worthy of the god of wine and pleasure himself. Alexander received bad news that stunned him, however, when he moved westward in early 324 to Persis, the satrapy at the center of the empire: his treasurer Harpalus, a childhood friend and extravagant spendthrift whom Alexander had previously pardoned for misappropriating royal funds, had fled from Babylon with 5,000 talents of the king's money and 6,000 mercenaries, leaving behind a temple that he had built at enormous cost to Alexander's treasury to commemorate Harpalus' beautiful and sexually alluring female companions. This betrayal staggered the king.

The emotional roller coaster continued. News came that the fleet had at last made it through, and Alexander rushed off to meet Nearchus, who had hurried inland with his closest attendants. The king nearly failed to recognize his admiral, haggard from the treacherous voyage, and when he saw the small company that attended this seeming beggar, Alexander broke down in tears, thinking that these few were all that survived. Nearchus quickly reassured him that nearly all of the ships and men had returned safely, and Alexander exulted. Nearchus had an amazing story to tell of the fleet's adventures: on shore, they had met the Fish-Eaters, a Stone Age tribe that ate fish raw and lived in huts made from the bones of giant sea creatures; at sea, they had seen a school of whales whose water spouting struck terror into his sailors, who thought they had blundered into a herd of sea monsters. Nearchus' vivid written account of this voyage, worthy of Odysseus, later became a "best-selling" book.

§6.

By February 324, Alexander was back in Susa, one of the ancient Persian capitals. When he heard that the tomb at Pasargadae of Cyrus, the first Persian king, had been plundered and the body treated disrespectfully, he ordered the monument restored to its glory. He gave awards to those of his men who had distinguished themselves on the eastern campaign and gave gold crowns (traditional signs of outstanding personal excellence) to select commanders, including his closest friend Hephaestion, his naval commander Nearchus, and Peucestas, one of the men who risked his own life to save Alexander when the king jumped off the wall into the midst of the Malli in India. Alexander also staged a spectacular occasion that reinforced the message of his punishment of corrupt satraps and powerfully expressed his commitment as a new kind of being (a mixture of the human and the divine) to establishing a new kind of empire – a government in which the upper hierarchy of power was defined by a "mixed" culture. For five days both Greek and Indian entertainers put on shows.

The culmination of the celebration took place in the world's largest tent, a giant structure a half-mile around hung with luxurious carpets and supported by columns thirty feet high, shining with gold and jewels. In this setting erected in the opulent style of the Persian Great King, Alexander led ninety prominent Macedonians and Greeks, his Companions, in marrying Persian women according to the protocols of Persian weddings. Alexander and Hephaestion married daughters of Darius to link their lineages to the Persian royal house. (Alexander also remained married to Roxane, in the polygamous tradition of Macedonian kings.) Alexander presented rich dowries to all the brides. These marriages at Susa, all arranged by Alexander, sent an unmistakable message: going forward in Alexander's world, power would belong to those who endorsed "mixing" barbarian and non-barbarian (i.e., Greek and Macedonian) cultures. Aristotle's teacher, Plato, had written a dialogue in which Socrates repeated a speech he said that he had learned from a famous Greek woman, whose words equated Greek pride, patriotism, and purity with hating barbarians and explicitly damned the "mixing" of the two "races." Alexander now rejected this view in the most public way possible, just as he had ignored Aristotle's advice to treat barbarians as slaves and animals. He was more than willing to rule barbarians – and everybody else – but experience had taught him that, just as knowledge could be found anywhere, so, too, individuals of superior excellence existed in all peoples. He intended to make use of them to further his plans, if they maintained their loyalty and supported his policy of "mixture."

§7.

One such supporter was Peucestas. He, like Alexander, had begun to wear Persian clothing, and alone of the army commanders had learned to speak Persian. Alexander appointed him satrap of Persis, the most symbolically important of the new empire's regions. To show that his policy could bring benefits to everyone, not just the elite, Alexander presented wedding presents to some 10,000 of his soldiers who had taken wives from the local populations along the way. His changes also directly altered the foundation of his power: the nature of his army. In spring 324, he introduced those he entitled the Successors, the 30,000 young Persians that had been trained under his command to speak Greek and fight like Macedonian warriors. They were brought onto the parade ground to demonstrate their military skills. This show, on top of the title Successors, made the Macedonian veterans worry that the king was aiming to replace them. Alexander also reorganized the Companion cavalry to include more barbarian horsemen, taking the very best of them into the elite unit that served as his mounted guard. Alexander realized that these changes would upset many of his men, and he made a grand gesture to remind them that he continued to do what he thought was best for them: he announced that he would pay off every debt, no matter how large, that anyone had incurred on the eastern expedition. Since many soldiers had in fact spent everything they had made and borrowed much more, this was a spectacular offer. At first almost no one admitted to having any debts, for fear that the king was tricking them into admitting to misbehavior for which he would punish them. He then reproached them with the pointed remark that a king must tell the truth – surely a sentiment from his long reflections on what it meant to be a ruler ruling with excellence – and paid off every claim with no proof of the amount owed.

§8.

Then, in mid-324, Alexander returned his attention to the Greek city-states. His last personal contact with them was now ten years in the past, and the orders he issued showed them that much had changed in how the "leader by consensus" of the alliance of "The Greeks" saw himself and them. First, he sent a proclamation that was read publicly to the Greeks assembled for the Olympic Games in the Peloponnese. Alexander announced that the Greeks must welcome back to their home cities all men previously sent away in exile, except those convicted of murder or sacrilege. These exiles congregated in various locations across Europe and Asia, gangs of homeless, angry, and armed men legally excluded from their hometowns. Their ranks were now swollen with the former mercenaries cut loose from employment by Alexander's re-establishment of order in his Asian empire. Some of these men were deserters from either Persian or Macedonian armies, or from the mixed settlements Alexander had founded across the route of his conquests. They all represented a threat to public order, potential criminals or pirates or, worse, the nucleus of a ready-made mercenary army that a rebellious coalition of city-states could employ to resist Alexander's rule. An order that the Greeks accept the exiles' return and restore their property would disperse this threat, but not without causing other problems. How would each city restore confiscated property, which had gone to other owners? What about vendettas of revenge over the crimes that had led to a sentence of exile? Alexander's "Exiles Decree" also violated the letter of the agreement that his father, Philip II, had originally made with the Greeks assembled at Corinth: the alliance of "The Greeks" and its hegemon would not meddle in the internal affairs of each member-city. Nevertheless, Alexander announced that he was going to enforce this order.

§9.

The next official notice from Alexander was a request, not a demand, but it was even more shocking to most people. He wrote to the Greek states asking each of them to grant him the honors due a divinity. This was not an order to declare him a god, not quite. But any fine distinction made no difference at all to Alexander's prominent opponents among the Greeks. At Athens Demosthenes sneered, "Alexander can be the son of Zeus, and of Poseidon as well, if that's what he wants." At Sparta Damis remarked dismissively, "Since Alexander desires to be a god, well then, let him be a god." The official responses were much less condescending. Officially, the Greeks took the request seriously. The democratic assembly governing Athens debated a motion to set up a statue of "King Alexander Unbeatable God," a title that reveals the official recognition that the Athenians believed they were expected to give. Athens and other Greek city-states dispatched representatives to Alexander, instructed to greet the king as was fitting for envoys on a sacred mission. (The delegations reached him at Babylon in the spring of 323.) Greeks had traditionally praised extraordinary individuals by calling them "god-like," and Philip had of course had his own statue carried into the stadium with those of the Olympian gods on the day he was assassinated. But the worship of Alexander was something new. Dionysus, first born human then reborn divine, and Heracles, divinized after his death, were human beings who had become gods, but Alexander was a god who walked among human beings, while remaining himself a human being as well. That is the point of a famous incident that is usually interpreted to mean that Alexander, against all the evidence to the contrary, denied his own divinity. Once when one of the scholars in Alexander's entourage saw the king's blood spouting from a war wound, he remarked with a quotation from the *Iliad*, "That is ichor, such as flows in the veins of the gods!" Alexander replied, "No, that's blood."

In other words, Alexander was not a god like those described by Homer and Hesiod, deities who had inherited their divine nature without having to earn it through struggle, labor, and pain without limit, striving and achieving and suffering on the earth among human beings, as a human being. Alexander was a man who became a god by going beyond all his predecessors through his achievements, by proving his surpassing excellence. He was in the end a mixed being, with a mixed nature – and therefore a better, stronger, more powerful nature, as Aristotle had taught. Alexander's teacher had explained in his analysis of the process of change that when different things were made more equal in their powers and mixed, one thing was not changed into the other, thereby losing its identity; instead, the new reality was "in between" and "shared." A "better nature" emerged. This philosophical definition of "mixing" describes as well as any the theoretical motivation for Alexander's policy and his vision of himself. As Plutarch concluded, of all of Alexander's equipment, the most important for his expedition was his training in philosophical reasoning. Alexander believed that he proved the truth of Aristotle's analysis of a "mixed" nature more so than any human being in history.

As far as Alexander was concerned, his status so greatly surpassed that of any other human being, past or present, that only new and unique conditions could reflect the new and unique reality that he was creating. This does not imply, as has sometimes been suggested in modern scholarship, that Alexander meant, either speciously or genuinely, to use a claim of divinity as some kind of narrow legal justification for his new relationship with the Greeks (or anyone else). His justification, if that is the right concept, stemmed from what he had learned about himself and his world, through his deep immersion in ways of thought going back to Homer's *Iliad* and through the unprecedented accomplishments of his career over the years. He, and what he had done, stood as the unique culmination of the excellence that in his experience and his imagination defined everything of value. It was now up to others to come to the same realization and, over time, adapt their behavior toward him accordingly.

§ 10.

Alexander had no intention of resting on his laurels, waiting for the world to catch up to his own vision of reality. Another *pothos* seized him. He would explore the Persian Gulf. His work on the east-west sea route continued; he had another Alexandria built on the coast as a trading center. He improved river travel on the Tigris by removing outdated barriers to navigation, and he scouted the region in preparation for a new military campaign into Arabia. When he reached the city of Opis on the Tigris, he made another major announcement: he was sending home all the troops whose age or injuries made them unfit for hard duty. Each man would receive a lavish bonus, ensuring a comfortable retirement. The army was furious: "Fire us all!" the men shouted, "You can keep on fighting with the help of your 'father'!" Where Alexander intended a generous rest from long service, his men saw the end of the Macedonian army that had fought so hard, for so long. Now, they thought, even more Persian Successors were going to serve the king, share in victories, and reap rewards. These Macedonians were Alexander's men, and like their king they could stand toil, pain, injury, and death with grim determination, but at any hint of betrayed trust they flew into a passion. Their mutinous anger arose from their anxiety, but their mockery of Alexander's belief in his divine parent proved a terrible misjudgment. The king immediately flew into a rage, leaped down from the speaker's platform, and ordered the leading complainers arrested and executed as traitors. He launched into a bitter speech, upbraiding his soldiers as disgracefully ungrateful. Hadn't he, and his father before him, done everything to make their homeland powerful, their lives successful, their families rich, their names immortal? He finished with a stinging rebuke: "So, go home; tell everyone there that you abandoned your king among barbarians. That report will surely win you praise from men and reward from gods. Go!" He then locked himself in his quarters, eating nothing and admitting no one. The soldiers still refused to back down, until he announced that Persians would now make up his elite units as his Companions, and that only those "members of his family" would be allowed to kiss him (as the symbol of the closest possible bond between ruler and ruled).

This broke the soldiers' will. They surrounded his chambers until he emerged to forgive them, saying "I make all of you members of my family." To seal the reconciliation, he then hosted a banquet for 9,000 guests. Alexander sat the leading Macedonians next to himself, then the leading Persians, and then the leaders of the "other peoples." The celebration climaxed with Alexander's libation and prayer that there would be "harmony and sharing in rule between Macedonians and Persians." In the aftermath, he followed through with his original plan and sent the veterans off to Macedonia, each with a huge payment. He advised them to leave their children from local women with him, to avoid trouble with their families back home, promising to raise their mixed-ethnic offspring and to arrange reunions when they had grown up. To lead the discharged veterans home he appointed Craterus, with orders to replace Antipater as his agent overseeing Greece. Alexander's motivation for ordering such a significant change of command is unclear. Some scholars speculate that Alexander had by now become almost pathologically suspicious and wanted Antipater removed so that he could not threaten the king's prominence by taking over Macedonia and Greece to rule as his own; Alexander's mother Olympias had written him letters accusing Antipater of just that treachery.

Whatever was going on behind the scenes, Antipater gave no sign that he had any hostility to Alexander. He even sent his son Cassander as a visitor to Alexander's court in Asia in early 323. As it happened, Craterus never delivered his message to Antipater, and so we cannot know if the old general in Greece would have surrendered his long-held position in Europe and made the journey to Asia and Alexander.

§ 11.

Alexander was in Babylon now, continuing to plan his Arabian expedition, and he was struck by the worst blow of his life: Hephaestion, his closest friend since childhood, died after a week of feverish disease made worse by dehydration from drinking wine. The most famous Greek medical expert of the past, Hippocrates, had recommended wine as a treatment for fever, but some sources say that Hephaestion took this treatment to extremes, consuming far too much alcohol. When the news reached Alexander, the king collapsed in grief. He had recently made Hephaestion his second-in-command of the empire, and he profoundly needed his Companion's emotional and political support. The depth of Alexander's devastation at his death reflected this need, but it also reflected the cumulative stress of the past two years, beginning with the refusal of the army to go beyond the Hyphasis River, to his near fatal wound in India, to the heart-wrenching losses of the march through the Gedrosian Desert, to the disloyalty of the satraps and of the army at Opis. In his grief he ordered the death of Hephaestion's doctor, a penalty for malpractice, and he ordered a cult to be established for his dead friend; he sent an embassy to Ammon's oracle in Egypt to ask whether the worship should be of a hero or a god. He hired the architect who had laid out the original Alexandria to design an enormous tomb 600 feet long on each side and 200 feet high, at a cost of more than 10,000 talents, which was roughly five times as much as the Athenians had spent a century before on the spectacular buildings including the Parthenon that made their Acropolis so famous.

§12.

For Alexander, only action could ease pain and erase memories, and in the winter of 324 – 323 he led a force against a mountain tribe that had perpetually defied the Persian king, even going so far as to demand payment of tolls for passage through their territory. Shrugging off the hardships of cold weather and high altitudes, Alexander forced their submission after a campaign of only forty days. He returned to Babylon and kept a hectic schedule of planning and preparations. He sent orders to the shipyards, laying keels for an even greater fleet to support his Arabian mission, and he dispatched explorers to map the coastline and prepare reports on plants and animals. He sent surveying expeditions by sea to measure the breadth of the Arabian peninsula; this forbidding body of land was to be the linchpin of a route connecting India and Egypt. Even beyond these immediate and ambitious plans he looked north and west. He commissioned other ships for exploration in the vast Caspian Sea to the north. When ambassadors arrived from western lands – Carthage and North Africa, western Europe and perhaps even Rome, he welcomed them and their proposals for new political relations. In time he planned to take his army to the extreme west, following the footsteps of Heracles so as to find the way to "go beyond" that man-become-god.

Western allies and the intelligence they could offer about routes, challenges, and particularly the city of Rome, a growing power in Italy, suited Alexander's far-reaching vision of the future. He had read in Herodotus that Queen Semiramis had improved the channels of the Euphrates River, and he set his engineers to improving those works. He laid out plans for another city of Alexandria on the Euphrates. When Peucestas, satrap of Persis, arrived in Babylon with 20,000 soldiers collected from the local peoples of the empire, Alexander integrated these men into his army by reorganizing the traditional phalanx. His fighting unit of infantry would now have twelve Persian spearmen in each column of sixteen men, with three

Macedonians at the head of the line and one at the rear. Through this reform, the paradigm of "mixing" would literally extend from the royal court to the front line of battle.

§13.

The messengers returned from the oracle of Zeus Ammon in Egypt: the god had answered that the cult of Hephaestion should be to honor a hero. Alexander could now bury his friend. He held a funeral ceremony at which 10,000 animals were sacrificed. Following this offering to the gods and to his dead Companion, it seemed to many that the gods spoke to Alexander again, twice, with ominous messages. As he sailed on the Euphrates River, a gust of wind blew off his diadem, the band of fabric designating Persian kingship. A sailor jumped into the water to retrieve it, and in trying to keep it dry as he swam back to the ship, the man placed it around his own head. Alexander rewarded the man for this service, and then put him to death, because the Babylonian prophets saw the event – the diadem on another's head – as an omen promising a new king. Shortly thereafter, a man, possibly demented – and madness was seen as sent from the gods – wandered into the royal chamber, donned Alexander's royal robes, and sat on his throne. On the advice of religious experts this man, too, met his death. Plutarch, familiar with omens, reverence to the gods, and the interpretation of signs, says that Alexander overreacted, allowing superstition and paranoia to override justice. Perhaps the king was deteriorating mentally and emotionally, or perhaps he was acting consistently and according to his character, stopping at nothing to align himself with the goodwill of the gods in pursuit of superhuman excellence.

In this case, the Babylonian prophets and their interpretations proved correct. In late May of 323, as Alexander was ready to set out for Arabia on a new quest around the world, he fell ill with a fever. Like Hephaestion, he followed the advice of the great Hippocrates and treated his fever with wine. Like his friend, he acted on the assumption that if a little was good, more was better, and very much more was best of all. He drank heavily at two parties in succession, and collapsed into his bed. His strength failed. His men panicked and forced their way into his room to see him. Too weak to speak to them, Alexander could only raise his head and blink his eyes to greet them. The Babylonians were meticulous astronomers, and their calendars were excellent, and so we know that on the evening of June 10, 323, Alexander died.

§14.

Some sources say that he had been poisoned on the initiative of Antipater, or even through a plot by Aristotle; others deny it. The simplest explanation is a bad fever, made worse by exhaustion, and made fatal by dehydration. Diodorus reports that on his deathbed Alexander removed his signet ring, the sign of his office, and handed it to his general Perdiccas. When his friends, gathered with him in his last moments, asked to whom he was leaving the throne of empire, he said, "To the man who is *kratistos* (the best and most powerful)." In Greek literature, Zeus was *kratistos* of all the gods, and Achilles was *kratistos* of all warriors. The superlative power of the *kratistos* was more than physical; it was intellectual and rhetorical, like that of Themistocles, the Greek commander who had outsmarted the Persian king Xerxes during the invasion, almost two centuries earlier, that Alexander had now avenged. As Alexander had learned from reading Thucydides, this term expressed the supreme level of excellence for Greeks. The historian had portrayed Pericles, the most famous leader of Athens in its most famous era at the culmination of the most famous speech he ever gave, telling the Athenians that they all must strive to deserve that status. The *kratistos* had to be the most effective fighter, the most insightful thinker, the best planner, and the most persuasive speaker. The excellence that marked a man as *kratistos* belonged, in Alexander's mind and heart, to the better, stronger, more powerful natures that Aristotle had praised. It was the nature that emerged from mixing, and that was Alexander's ideal.

10

REMEMBERING AND JUDGING ALEXANDER (323 BC TO NOW)

§ I.

No one met Alexander's ideal; none of his companions, events showed, measured up to the standard of being *kratistos*. When Alexander died, he left detailed plans for grand schemes that would unify his empire and expand it, a mixed realm ruled by Macedonians, Greeks, and capable men of any nation loyal to his vision. The plans included a thousand warships, larger than any ever seen, for a naval expedition to North Africa, Sicily, and Spain; they described a road, equipped with ports and ship-yards, stretching from Egypt to the Pillars of Heracles, where the Mediterranean met the Atlantic; six great temples would be erected in Greece and Macedonia; finally – the culmination of a vision of a mixed culture redefining power in the world – his plans called for new cities as homes for populations transferred from Asia to Europe and from Europe to Asia. As Diodorus reports, Alexander intended through intermarriages and home-steads, "to put the greatest continents into a partnership of har-mony and love based on family ties." Perdiccas presented all of these plans to the assembled army. The soldiers agreed with his judgment that they were too difficult and too expensive. Not a single one was carried out. The generals all proclaimed their support for Alexander's family, pledging to support his impaired brother, who would share the kingship with the child soon to be born to Alexander's pregnant wife, if the baby was male. Behind these empty words they were all frantically crafting their own schemes and promoting their own narrow interests.

Everything fell apart. Every leading Macedonian but one immediately divorced the Persian wife he had married at Susa. With the exception of some barbarian troops remaining in the armies – and there was no longer a single army, but many forces, each under the command of a different general and serving private ends – there was no more talk of "mixing." Within a year the splintered fragments of Alexander's army of conquest turned into warring factions. The chaos lasted two decades. In this period every member of Alexander's family, including his mother, was put to death, and internecine wars fractured his empire into sections that his former commanders captured and ruled for themselves. By the end of the fourth century, these victors declared themselves kings. The Successors, as they are called, founded dynasties that would dominate the political and military history of Greece, Egypt, and southwest Asia for more than 200 years, until the Romans conquered them in the second and first centuries BC. Of these dynasties, those of Ptolemy in Egypt and Seleucus in the Near East lasted the longest and held the most power, although neither ever had the ambition to rival the extent of Alexander's conquests. Seleucus, in fact, traded away the satrapies of India and Afghanistan to Chandragupta, the founder of the Maurya Empire in India; Seleucus received in exchange a diplomatic marriage and 500 war elephants. These new kingdoms were Hellenistic ("Greek-like"), with Greeks and Macedonians in power over locals in government and society; the last queen of the Ptolemaic dynasty, Cleopatra VII (69–30 BC), was the first of her line to learn to speak Egyptian (and other languages native to her subjects).

§ 2.

In short, the new world that Alexander had begun and hoped to extend did not survive his death. The fame that he had pursued so passionately, however, lived on; indeed it continued to expand. It is unknown when he was first called "the Great," but it seems not to have been during his lifetime. The earliest attestation of that epithet appears in a Roman comedy by Plautus from the second century BC, but modern scholars have suggested that Ptolemy called Alexander "the Great" when he stole his corpse and its casket as it was being transported back home to Macedonia. Ptolemy built a tomb for his dead king in Alexandria in Egypt, the capital of the land he had seized for himself. His possession of the mortal remains of this superhuman king was a symbol of the legitimacy he sought for his own dynasty. Ptolemy and his son followed Alexander's example, too, by asserting the duty of kings to seek and promote knowledge. In their capital of Alexandria they built a state-funded research foundation: the Museum, an institute dedicated to the Muses, goddesses of knowledge and culture. They hired professional scholars to take up residence there, and they paid for a library whose mission was to acquire a copy of every book in the world.

The most widely distributed and read "texts" in the world were the images and words on coins, and Ptolemy took full advantage of this to advertise his symbolic connection with the great Alexander. He minted various denominations bearing portraits of Alexander, including one in which the conqueror wears an elephant skull headdress and has the horns characteristic of Zeus Ammon curling out from his temple. These coins delivered a message that the ever-victorious and divine spirit of Alexander validated and protected Ptolemy's rule over Egypt. Other Hellenistic rulers, and later many Greek cities in the eastern Roman empire, followed this example, putting Alexander on their coins and thus claiming a share in his legend. This tradition continued for 800 years.

§ 3.

The Romans were fascinated by Alexander, whom some saw as a source of inspiration, some as an example to shun. A staple of Roman education and philosophy was the debate over Alexander – should men strive to be like him or reject his model? Julius

Caesar famously lamented that his own achievements were nothing compared to those of Alexander at the same age. Other Romans were strongly critical. The philosopher Seneca acknowledged that Alexander's "longing" transcended mere human lust or greed, but he expressed horror at the deaths that Alexander caused. To the epic poet Lucan, Alexander was an insane tyrant in love with slaughter, whom an avenging Fate destroyed for his crimes. Roman teachers assigned their advanced students to give presentations such as "Would Alexander make this decision or that? What contributed most to Alexander's victories, excellence or luck? What limits should there be to ambition?"

Alexander's example continued to inspire the emperors who ruled for centuries after the fall of the Republic. Trajan (ruled AD 98–117) led a Roman army into Mesopotamia, in the footsteps of Alexander. When he reached the shores of the Persian Gulf, the emperor looked wistfully eastward and remarked that he wished he was young enough to emulate Alexander's expedition to India. Caracalla (ruled AD 209–217) revered Alexander so much that when he put his own image on his coins, the image was holding a shield bearing a portrait of Alexander. Caracalla was waging war in the Near East against the Parthians who were reviving the Persian Empire; the Roman emperor hoped that by honoring his idol, who had never lost against Persian armies, he might gain Alexander's aid. The emperor and author Julian the Apostate (ruled AD 361–363), who also commanded a military expedition to Mesopotamia, believed himself to be Alexander, a living body playing host to the transmigrated soul of the legendary Macedonian. It was not only Roman rulers who took Alexander as a model: Sultan Alauddin Jhali (ruled AD 1296–1316), who created a vast empire in medieval India, inscribed his coins with the title "The Second Alexander." To add legitimacy to his dynasty, the first Muslim ruler of Malacca (Malaya) in the Indian Ocean claimed Alexander as his ancestor.

The emperor Julian had depicted Alexander, alongside famous Roman emperors, in his fictional dialogue *The Caesars*. And it was fiction like this that did the most to spread Alexander's reputation across the world. Popularized accounts of Alexander's life and deeds appeared very soon after his death, and they have continued to be written and have found enthusiastic audiences ever since. For centuries these diverse retellings were based on a Greek work that today carries the title *The Alexander Romance*. The *Romance* included genuine historical facts, some of which appear in no other accounts, but it was mostly a deeply imaginative tale of adventure and marvels. It offered a picture of Alexander as a man of courage and competitive ambition for excellence, and with a desire for knowledge, but its narrative interwove actual events with entertaining fictions that often carried moral lessons on how to live. In the *Romance*, Alexander explores the depths of the ocean in a crystal diving bell, flies through the skies in a basket borne aloft by eagles, fights monsters, consults an oracle in the form of a magical tree, finds the Water of Life that confers immortality (but refuses to drink it), and is turned back from the Islands of the Blessed by two human-headed birds speaking Greek. Though mixing its tales with historical material, the *Romance* sometimes altered the record; it said that Alexander was the son of the Egyptian pharaoh Nectanebo, and that he killed king Porus in man-to-man single combat. The *Romance* became incredibly popular, translated into more than twenty languages. It was known and loved in areas Alexander never came near; it inspired, among others, the bards of western Africa to compose musical epic poems about the hero Sunjata.

§4.

The *Romance* was translated into every major language of Europe and the Near East. During the Roman Empire, it was translated into Latin so that Europeans ignorant of Greek could read it – this honor was accorded to few works of Greek history, not Herodotus, not Thucydides. An early translation was produced in Syriac, a Semitic literary language that was widespread in the Near East in late antiquity; this version, in turn, inspired accounts of Alexander in Arabic, Persian, and Hebrew. Early Islamic scholars identified Alexander with the person called

"The Two-Horned One" in the *Qur'an* (seventh century AD), who travels to the end of the world in the East and the West and uses the power given to him by God to construct an iron wall to block the evil Gog and Magog. Medieval Arabic texts included sayings attributed to Alexander as a philosopher and an exchange of letters with Aristotle on the principles for ruling as a king. A Persian Zoroastrian text from late antiquity condemned him as "Alexander the Accursed," but medieval Persian epic poets composed elaborate narratives that rehabilitated him. Firdausi (or Ferdowsi, AD 940–1020), author of the *Shahnamah*, the national epic poem of Iran, made him the son of a Persian king and therefore a legitimate heir to the Persian throne. Nezami (AD 1141–1209) portrayed Alexander as a great general, whose conquests extended to Russia and China, and who embarked on a quest for knowledge, becoming first an ideal ruler and then a prophet, traveling the world to preach monotheistic religion. Nestorian Christians, fleeing east to escape religious persecution from other Christians in the late Roman Empire, brought stories of Alexander with them to central Asia, which later inspired a Mongol version of the *Romance*. Alexander first appeared in Jewish tradition in the work of the first-century AD historian Flavius Josephus, who described Alexander as coming to Jerusalem and meeting with the High Priest of the Temple. "Alexander the Macedonian" later appeared in legendary tales in the Talmud and Midrash; in one story, Alexander announces that he always had the image of the Jewish high priest carried with him into battle to ensure victory.

§ 5.

Stories in Latin about Alexander's time in India became particularly popular in Europe. They were filled with colorful descriptions of the many marvels of the East, from natural wonders such as a river of honey to fabulous creatures such as the Dog Heads, who had human bodies dressed in animal skins but with the heads of dogs and who were unable speak human language, only bark; or the Odontotyrannus ("Toothed Tyrant"), a huge amphibian with three horns and a mouth big enough to swallow an elephant whole. These narratives also focused on Alexander as a seeker of knowledge in this land of (to Europeans) exotic wisdom, conversing with Brahman wise men. The Indians' philosophically and morally directed conversations compared Alexander's relentlessly active way of thought and life with their contemplative and ascetic beliefs and practices, including vegetarianism.

The idea that Indian sages converted Alexander into a man of wisdom contributed to another reinvention, this time in Christian literature. There, he became "the believing Alexander," a pious worshipper of God and a promoter of peace. In some versions, he was even made a Christian saint. His piety, in these Christian treatments, stemmed from his being the first man to find his way to a divinely protected land that was seen as Paradise on Earth, or at least as a Purgatory City for souls on their way to heaven. He was not allowed to enter, but he was given a sparkling jewel that was also a human eye. Through the advice of religious teachers, he came to understand that the eye was leading him to give up his longing for ever more accomplishment and the never-satisfied desire for fame, and to choose a peaceful and quiet life helping others.

These fantasies only made Alexander an even more popular figure of legend in Europe. French, German, and English romances of the Middle Ages told stories of Alexander as the ideal medieval knight behaving with the ultimate chivalry, fighting valiant battles against Saracens (Muslims) and involved in romantic entanglements with ladies at court. In Geoffrey Chaucer's *Canterbury Tales*, it is said that every living creature with any awareness at all had heard some or all of the fortune of Alexander the Great. The notion that Alexander's fame could provide legitimacy for anyone connected to him, which Ptolemy had first tried to exploit, had still not died out 1,700 years later: the late medieval French romance, *Perceforest*, describes Alexander being blown by a storm at sea from India to Britain, where he establishes one of his generals as king of Britain and another as king of Scotland, making the Macedonian

conqueror the ancestor of ancient royalty there, including King
Arthur.

§6.

Nevertheless, the ancient tradition of rejecting Alexander as a
role model also persisted in early modern times. William Shake-
speare in his tragic drama *Hamlet* (written around 1600) has
the Danish prince conclude that Alexander's achievements in
the end made him nothing more than the raw material for glue:
"Alexander died, Alexander was buried, Alexander returneth
into dust, the dust is earth, of earth we make loam and why
of the loam, whereto he was converted, might they not stop
a beer-barrel?" An especially striking example of the denigra-
tion of Alexander in English thought comes in Henry Fielding's
ironically titled novel *The History of the Life of the Late Mr.
Jonathan Wild the Great* (1743). The novelist mocks writers
who, in his biting opinion, falsely equate greatness with good-
ness; authors on Alexander are the leading offenders in this
distortion of the truth:

> In the histories of Alexander and Caesar we are frequently, and
> indeed impertinently, reminded of their benevolence and gen-
> erosity, of their clemency and kindness. When the former had
> with fire and sword overrun a vast empire, had destroyed the
> lives of an immense number of innocent wretches, had scattered
> ruin and desolation like a whirlwind, we are told, as an example
> of his clemency, that he did not cut the throat of an old woman,
> and ravish her daughters, but was content with only undoing
> them.

Political leaders, like many literary authors, have up until the
present day employed Alexander as a moral example, sometimes
as one to reject, sometimes as one to imitate, always as one that
must be studied for life lessons. Napoleon Bonaparte, emperor
of France (1804–1815), lamented that he could not conquer as
much of the world as Alexander had, but John Adams, second
president of the United States (1797–1801), in his old age cited
the example of Alexander to instruct the officers-in-training of

the U.S. Military Academy concerning the true nature of their mission:

> Battles, victories, and conquests, abstracted from their only justifiable end, which is justice and peace, are the glory of fraud, violence, and usurpation. What was the glory of Alexander and Caesar? 'The glimmering' which those 'livid flames' in Milton 'cast, pale and dreadful,' or 'the sudden blaze,' which 'far around illumin'd Hell.'

In his *Autobiography*, Thomas Jefferson, the third U.S. president (1801–1809), was equally, if more concisely, critical of Alexander: "There are three epochs in history signalized by the extinction of national morality. The first was of the successors of Alexander, not omitting himself. The next the successors of the first Caesar, the third our own age."

§7.

The twentieth-century leader who, modern commentators often claim, not only did not follow the tradition of criticizing Alexander but in fact admired the Macedonian conqueror and aimed to imitate him, was Adolf Hitler, chancellor of Nazi Germany (1933–1945). This assertion, however, seems misleading. There is only one citation of Alexander in the two volumes of *Mein Kampf*, Hitler's discursive manifesto on his political ideas. This passing reference, in a chapter discussing "Eastern Orientation or Eastern Policy," implicitly dismisses the Macedonian's expedition to the east as nothing more than the giddy exploit of an adventurer:

> Our duty, the mission of the National Socialist Movement, is to bring our own people to that political insight, which sees their goal for the future as being not fulfilled in the intoxicating sensation of a new Alexander trek, but much more in the assiduous work of the German plow, for which the German sword needs only to provide the soil."

When he took power, Hitler found his offices hung with two tapestries that depicted Alexander; the dictator had them replaced with ones showing legendary German tribal heroes.

Franklin D. Roosevelt, president of the United States when Hitler was launching World War II, cited Alexander as a negative example, in a press conference in April 1941 urging the American people to reject the idea that Hitler could not be stopped:

> I read an editorial on Monday, or something like that the other day – which said in effect, Why, we have always had conquerors all through the history of the world, and Alexander the Great who tried to conquer all the known world, he was not satisfied to stay at home – where was it, Macedonia? – he went out and tried to conquer lots of people he never saw before, just to add to his empire. He was not satisfied with his own people, his own flesh and blood. ... Now, coming back to this mythical person in our midst who takes the attitude that dictatorships are going to win anyway ... I don't think along those lines, and neither do you.

§8.

More recent political leaders have continued to pull references to Alexander from their toolboxes of useful historical examples, but usually with less of an edge. George H. W. Bush when president of the United States (1989–1993) once encouraged a group of youth leaders to action by remarking,

> Sometimes we adults forget the capability of young people to change the world, but you should remind all of us that youth is no barrier to great achievements. Knowing I was coming over here, I asked for some examples from history. ... [B]y the age of 32, Alexander the Great's empire stretched from Indiana – [Laughter.] – it included Indiana – from India to the Adriatic.

The current war in Afghanistan being fought by the United States and NATO forces has especially encouraged politicians to continue citing Alexander, at least in passing. In 2009, for example, Hillary Clinton remarked that when I think about my trips to Afghanistan, my flying over that terrain, my awareness of the history going back to Alexander the Great and, certainly, the imperial British military and Rudyard Kipling's memorable poems about Afghanistan, the Soviet Union, which put in more troops than we're thinking about putting in – I mean, it calls for a large dose of humility about what it is we are trying to accomplish.

Alexander also continues to appear as a headline in the controversies over nationalism in the Balkan Peninsula. The Hellenic Democracy (the modern nation of Greece) and the Republic of Macedonia (which declared its independence from the former Yugoslavia in 1991) fiercely dispute which is entitled to claim the territorial and ethnic name "Macedonia." Both, like Ptolemy more than 2,000 years ago, also claim a close connection to Alexander as a symbol of their political legitimacy. The erection in 2011 in Skopje, the capital of the Republic of Macedonia, of a huge bronze statue of Alexander riding his warhorse Bucephalas has heightened the tension, despite the official title of the monument as "A Warrior on a Horse." A poll of Greeks in 2010 designated Alexander as the "greatest Greek of all time," and he serves as an icon of Hellenic pride, at home and abroad. At the 2010 celebration in Washington, D.C. of Greek Independence Day, President Barack Obama commented,

Last year, His Eminence [Archbishop of the Oxthodox Church] tried to compare me with Alexander the Great. [Laughter] I thought this would get me more respect from Michelle and the girls. [Laughter] It did not. [Laughter] They reminded me instead that Greek literature is full of very strong women. [Laughter].

§9.

Alexander's reputation has lived on – and been frequently reinterpreted – in modern entertainment. In the mid-1990s, the BBC journalist Michael Wood made a 20,000-mile trek across seventeen countries to retrace the route of Alexander, an amazing journey vividly chronicled in a video and book, *In the Footsteps* of *Alexander the Great: A Journey from Greece to Asia*. He reports having encountered a remarkable diversity of oral storytellers spinning tales of Alexander and the wonders the Macedonian experienced on his expedition to the East so long before. From Greece to Pakistan, people in the late twentieth century still remembered Alexander, sometimes even claiming descent from the legendary hero. In music, Alexander has been the subject of compositions from classical to rock: the eighteenth-century composer George Frideric Handel wrote a piece on the theme of Alexander's infamously drunken party at Persepolis, plus operas on Alexander's relationship with Porus and his idea that he was a god. The British heavy metal band Iron Maiden put out an 8.5-minute song in 1986 titled "Alexander the Great," whose lyrics narrated his career complete with dates, quoted Plutarch, and repeated the chorus "Alexander the Great, His name struck fear into the hearts of men, Alexander the Great, Became a legend 'mongst mortal men."

Alexander's story has also inspired filmmakers. Their approaches have reflected their shared goal of entertaining their audiences, but also their differing aims in expressing messages relevant to their time and place. The Indian film *Sikandar* (1941), for example, portrays a youthful Alexander being awed by the nobility of King Porus, presented as the courageous defender of Indian freedom and dignity. Local commentators praised the movie for its acting, but even more for asserting Indian nationalism, at a time at the start of World War II when British colonial control of India was increasingly contested; the British banned *Sikandar* from being shown on their military bases in India. The 1965 Indian film *Sikander-e-Azam* was even more focused on using the story of Porus and Alexander to promote nationalist fervor. A half-century later in a different part of Asia, Alexander was the subject of a very modern treatment. *Reign: The Conqueror* (1999) is a Japanese-Korean anime video in thirteen episodes directed by Yoshinori Kanemori based on the novel *Alexander Senki* (*Alexander: The Record of his Battles*) by Hiroshi Aramata. The series retells Alexander's life as science fiction, with characters designed by Peter Chung in the same manga style that he used in *Aeon Flux* (originally broadcast on the MTV television network in the 1990s). The story line combines ancient history with a supernatural future, in which Alexander follows the personal quest laid out in the theme song: "Seek out a kingdom worthy of your soul!" As an updated *Alexander Romance*, the series infuses history with fantasy, such as making Bucephalas a wild beast that eats men alive but bonds with the "horse whisperer" Alexander, and having shape-shifting phantoms devoted to the philosopher Pythagoras stalk Alexander to try to destroy him.

American movies about Alexander belong to the two periods when "sword and sandal" epics were popular with Hollywood filmmakers, the mid-twentieth and early twenty-first centuries. *Alexander the Great* (1955), directed by Robert Rossen, emphasizes Alexander's early life and his conflict with his father, though it leaves ambiguous whether Alexander was behind Philip's murder. Like Plutarch's biography, the plot focuses on crucial episodes in Alexander's life and de-emphasizes battle scenes. Critics praised the film for its historical accuracy as a movie and for its complex characterizations, but found its speeches long-winded. A proposed 1968 TV series on Alexander starring William Shatner, which attempted to capitalize on the actor's newly won *Star Trek* fame, flopped when the pilot episode proved not only historically wildly inaccurate but also dull. *Alexander* (2004), directed by Oliver Stone, provoked energetic criticism from audiences, reviewers, and scholars, as well as the director himself, who reissued the film in two more versions to try to clarify its themes. The presentation of Olympias as weirdly superstitious and Alexander as hypersexualized aroused strong opposition; some were outraged in particular at the film's indications of homosexual activity by Alexander.

Both Rossen's 1955 film and Stone's twenty-first-century version portrayed Alexander as a proponent of the international policy called "The Unity of Mankind." This idea has been a touchstone in the fierce debate among modern scholars about Alexander's aims and the effects of his actions in the world, both intentional and unintentional. The vast and international range of modern scholarship on Alexander began in fierce earnest two centuries ago. From then until now, the pendulum of evaluation of Alexander has swung back and forth from admiration to condemnation, sometimes with a rush to judgment calibrated more by what are asserted to be contemporary standards of right and wrong than in the context of the ideas and practices of Alexander's own time. Some, especially those comparing Alexander to Hitler, have damned him as a megalomaniac, paranoid, and bloodthirsty murderer; Indian historians have been dismissive, writing him off as a passing inconvenience whose conquests were "meaningless" in the history of their subcontinent.

§ 10.

A persistent theme in the negative evaluations of Alexander is the notion that he behaved irrationally, especially in his actions to fulfill his "longing" to outdo Heracles and Dionysus and to achieve a new kind of divinity. But as the economic theorist Ludwig von Mises insists, it makes no sense to use the term "irrational" for purposive human action, that is, action aimed at a goal. An action undertaken in pursuit of a goal has purpose, whether the satisfaction of material needs or "higher" aims, such as religious belief or political freedom. Such action may be based on faulty reasoning, or mistaken information, but it is neither accurate nor useful to call it "irrational." If anything seems clear about Alexander, it is that he thought deeply about his actions, and he always acted with a purpose. In that fundamental sense, categorizing him as lacking rationality is itself an intellectually empty reproach. Alexander, like every other human being, made choices from a complex mixture of reasoning and emotion. He was a complex, even contradictory personality, which seems a given of human nature.

Many modern historians deny that Alexander's actions were based on ideals. This seems like a failure of historical imagination. Some scholars grant him the status of military genius and successful, pragmatic leader, based on the ancient sources, but ignore those very sources when they describe him as having a visionary foundation for his actions. Ernst Badian, the modern historian who engendered the evaluation of Alexander as essentially an irrational murderer lacking ideals, a view that A. B. Bosworth has even more forcefully advocated, commented scornfully that any other judgment is "romantic fiction," and that any attempt at an overall interpretation of his character is "worthless." These conclusions seem just as extreme, forced, and inadequate as does the account of Alexander written by William Woodthorpe Tarn. His meticulously detailed book, published in the hopeful years just after World War II, when the United Nations had just come into being, credited Alexander with the creation of a humanitarian doctrine of The Unity of Mankind and denied that Alexander ever did anything unworthy of a Victorian English gentleman, except once or twice.

§11.

Authors of a biography are obliged to evaluate their subject. In closing this biography, we offer this brief attempt at fulfilling our duty. Competition defined Alexander's life. He dedicated his three decades, above all, to the challenge of going beyond all others in excellence (*aretē*) and of winning the ultimate reward, a superhuman status that no human being had ever achieved. Alexander longed to become unique by becoming the best, and the religious concepts of his time convinced him that he could earn that fabulous distinction, that he could become not only, like the Achilles of Homer's *Iliad*, "the best of the Greeks," but the best of everyone, ever, anywhere, at any time. The values he lived – performance, respect, honor, and loyalty – were hard, with sharp edges that meant unhappy consequences for failures. Alexander also recognized and rewarded excellence in others, regardless of whether they were Macedonian, Greek, or barbarian, and he wanted to go beyond the violent parochialism of traditional Macedonian attitudes toward others by extending his policy of "mixing," from clothing to court protocols to military units to entire populations. With this policy, based on knowledge and experience, he aimed to implement his vision of an empire that would surpass anything ever seen before, with the new, better nature that "mixing" produced. He failed, of course. He died too soon to finish the mission he set for himself. Perhaps the mission was impossible. Perhaps human nature and the conditions of the world would have prevented him from fulfilling his vision, however long he had lived. Certainly every other such attempt in history has failed, too, for better or worse. To deny that Alexander held such an ideal seems unimaginable to us, since it is present and visible in every ancient source that describes the history of Alexander of Macedon.

The ideal we mention was not a vision of "unity" or, as Tarn also called it, "brotherhood" among peoples based on universal equality or sentimentality. Alexander did not believe in equality, and he was not sentimental. Alexander's ideal was ruthlessly competitive, violent to the disloyal or unconvinced, and supremely prideful. Still, there was in this ideal some notion that human beings were, or at least ideally should be, in some basic sense united in their humanness and the possibility of achieving excellence, even if they were not equal, could never be equal, and should never be equal. This idea of human unity went all the way back to the beginnings of Greek thought, and even Aristotle (despite his views on barbarians) taught that humans shared a bond of affection, by nature, one with another.

§12.

The most insightful characterization of Alexander emerges, fittingly, from the analysis that Aristotle gives of what he calls a "Man of Great Soul" (*megalopsuchos*), the concept mentioned at the start of this biography. Diodorus and Plutarch apply this description to Alexander, but scholars of Aristotle today still debate how to interpret the philosopher's complex ideas on this category of extraordinary individuals. Philosophical debates aside, Aristotle's conception of this type of human being helps us see and understand Alexander in his own time and place. The Man of Great Soul recognizes his supreme standing among others and has no tolerance for insults. He becomes wildly angry at ungrateful and disloyal people. Craving knowledge, he employs practical thoughtfulness in everything that he does, and he endures misfortune. He is the greatest benefactor of others, and he deserves – and expects to receive – the greatest honor in return. Friendship is as important to him as is honor. His accomplishments raise him to the level of the gods.

By these criteria, Alexander was a Man of Great Soul. Aristotle tells us that such a man is the best, but he is not perfect; he can make mistakes in judgment. He is also not a man living a life of pure contemplation, the choice that Aristotle himself thought was the ideal. The Man of Great Soul is a man of action, with and for others; he is political, in the original ancient Greek sense of "belonging to and acting in and for a community of people." He is simultaneously among those people and above them. He achieves a wondrous life, in the dual sense of wonder that Herodotus says is the basis of history, wondrous in its positives and its negatives. So was Alexander wondrous, and we believe that he would approve our closing this account by recalling the words of Homer in the *Iliad,* the poem most precious to the Macedonian king. The poet says, of the great Achilles, that he strove with longing "always to be the best and to be eminent over the others."

SUGGESTED READINGS

For Arrian, Curtius, and Diodorus, and Plutarch, as well as Homer, Euripides, and Herodotus, the Loeb Classical Library editions (Cambridge, Mass.: Harvard University Press) offer readable English translations alongside the original language of the ancient sources. For Justin, see J. C. Yardley's translations: *Justin. Epitome of the Philippic History of Pompeius Trogus* (Atlanta: Scholars Press, 1994), and *Justin. Epitome of the Philippic History of Pompeius Trogus. Volume I. Books 11–12: Alexander the Great*. Commentary by Waldemar Heckel (Oxford: Oxford University Press, 1997). Charles A. Robinson, *The History of Alexander the Great*. Vol. 1 (Providence: Brown University, 1953) translates the "fragments" of the "lost" historians of Alexander, meaning quotations and paraphrases of earlier ancient sources found in later, surviving sources.

Modern studies of Alexander are overwhelmingly numerous and diverse. Waldemar Heckel and Lawrence A. Tritle, editors, *Alexander the Great: A New History* (Chichester, U.K. and Malden, Mass.: Wiley-Blackwell, 2009), pp. 311–348 provide an extensive bibliography. Waldemar Heckel, *Who's Who in the Age of Alexander the Great: Prosopography of Alexander's Empire* (Malden, Mass. and Oxford: Blackwell, 2006) gives short descriptions, including source citations, for many individuals known from the history of Alexander. The spectrum of modern interpretations of Alexander's personality and aims ranges from the visionary leader promoting the "brotherhood of man" imagined by William Woodthorpe Tarn in *Alexander the Great* (Cambridge: Cambridge University Press, 1948) to the near sociopath seemingly unable to sate his blood lust conceived by Ernst Badian in "Alexander the Great and the Loneliness of Power," in *Studies in Greek and Roman History* (Oxford: Oxford University Press, 1964), pp. 192–205, and by A. B. Bosworth in *Conquest and Empire: The Reign of Alexander the Great* (Cambridge: Cambridge University Press, 1988) and *Alexander and the East: The Tragedy of Triumph* New ed. (Oxford: Oxford University Press, 2004). For more balanced accounts, it is worth reading, from among many biographies that surely deserve mention in a longer list, Ulrich Wilcken, *Alexander the Great*. Trans. G. C. Richards with notes to Alexander studies by Eugene N. Borza (New York: Norton, 1967); J. R. Hamilton, *Alexander the Great* (Pittsburgh: University of Pittsburgh Press, 1974); Paul Cartledge, *Alexander the Great: The Hunt for a New Past* (London: Macmillan, 2004); Richard Stoneman, *Alexander the Great*. 2nd. ed. (London: Routledge, 2004); and Pierre Briant, *Alexander the Great and His Empire: A Short Introduction*. Trans. A. Kuhrt. (Princeton: Princeton University Press, 2010). Ian Worthington, *Alexander the Great: A Reader*. 2nd. ed. (London: Routledge, 2012) offers a combination of excerpts from ancient sources and modern scholarly interpretations.

INDEX